# *Water* FOR DRY PLACES

GAVIS MOSLEY

Copyright © 2017, 2018, 2019 by Gavis Mosley

All rights reserved. No part of this publication may be reproduced, distributed, or transmitted in any form or by any means, including photocopying, recording, or other electronic or mechanical methods, without the prior written permission of the publisher, except in the case of brief quotations embodied in critical reviews and certain other noncommercial uses permitted by copyright law.

The King James Version of the Holy Bible is in the public domain.

ISBN: 978-1-7336754-7-5

Liberation's Publishing LLC
West Point, Mississippi
www.liberationspublishing.com

# *Water* FOR DRY PLACES

GAVIS MOSLEY

Gavis Mosley

*You are my first love…*
*God the Father who created me…*
*Jesus the Christ who saved me…*
*the comforter, the gift, the Holy Spirit who keeps me.*
*You are the light out of darkness.*
*You are patience where there once lived compulsion.*
*You are peace where rage and confusion once reigned.*
*You are love, grace and mercy where anger, fear, guilt and shame once dominated*
*You are my first love.~*

*Psalms 16:11*
*~You make known to me the path of life; you will fill me with joy in your presence, with eternal pleasures at your right hand.*

## Table of Contents

A Mother's Cry ................................................................ 11

A Change Has Come! ..................................................... 15

A Means to Praise ........................................................... 19

A Plea for the Righteous ................................................ 23

A Prayer of Thanks ......................................................... 27

A Touch ............................................................................ 31

Accept What God Allows ............................................... 35

And David Danced .......................................................... 39

And Just Who Are You ................................................... 45

Angels Watching Over Me ............................................. 49

Ask God ............................................................................ 55

Be Encouraged ................................................................ 61

Believe God ..................................................................... 67

Be Strong in the Lord ..................................................... 73

Don't Look Back .............................................................. 77

Endow Me ........................................................................ 81

Enjoy the Journey ........................................................... 87

Forgive Me ....................................................................... 93

God's Hand ...................................................................... 97

God Will Provide ........................................................... 101

| | |
|---|---|
| Keeping Our Eyes on the Lord | 105 |
| More than Enough | 111 |
| You Kept Me | 115 |
| Open My Eyes | 119 |
| True Worship | 125 |
| Meditation of Daniel | 131 |
| Lesson Learned | 137 |
| I'm Afraid | 143 |
| How Deep Is Your Love? | 149 |
| Won't You Come? | 153 |
| About The Author | 159 |

Psalms 127:3
Lord, I thank you for your word.

"Lord, I thank for the manifestation of your promises in my life. Lord, your word tells me that "Children are a heritage from the Lord, offspring a reward from him." Lord, you know our journey, you know the challenges and the struggles. Yet, you have in your mighty wisdom, love and grace allowed us to overcome that which came to destroy us…you have worked all things together for our good

To my daughters with love…Virgilia Danielle, Kenya-Kanni Blake, and Triniti Aniya…I thank you for your enduring love and support. I thank you for being there when all else seemed to have fallen away. I thank you for continuing to stand on the word of God, in his strength, in his love.

Lord, I thank you for hearing A Mother's Cry.

To you my family, my friends, all those whom I encounter, and yes to those who proclaim to be my enemy…join me as I celebrate the goodness of the Lord in my life. What he had done for and in me, he so willingly and patiently awaits to do that and more for you. Won't You Come?

Gavis Mosley

# A MOTHER'S CRY

Father God, I thank you for hearing the prayer of a sincere heart. What are you believing God for? What has your heart and soul so torn that only God can do it or fix it for you? What is it? And as you pray, are you sincere? Do you truly believe that he will do it for you, or is there doubt in your heart? Have you checked your motives for asking for such a thing? Will it be to honor you or God? And then, can you or will you wait on the Lord? Are you able to endure trials and tribulations while you wait on the move of God? Will you remain faithful and continue to trust in him?
Go with me to 1 Samuel, chapter 1. During this era, it was important that a man have children. He wanted/needed them to carry on the family name. Therefore, sons were very crucial. So, if a man married a woman who could not have children, he would marry another woman as well. This often would cause trouble between the wives. In this day, a woman who was barren often felt shame and was looked upon as a failure.

So is the setting, as we look at Hannah. Hannah's husband, Elkanah was a man of God. At the appointed time, he and his entire family would go to the temple and worship. Elkanah loved Hannah very much. He knew her heart. He would give her a double portion to offer as a sacrifice to God. God had prevented her from having children. Hannah grieved her situation deeply, yet she loved the Lord with all her heart as she did her husband. One day they went to Shiloh. Everyone was celebrating…eating and drinking wine; all but Hannah. She was sad in her heart and deeply troubled. She not only had to deal with her own personal feelings of inadequacy and shame but she was faced daily with the ridicule of the other wife, who could bear children. Hannah was sad, her soul cried out to the Lord. She cried out from a sincere heart and a deep desire. She humbled herself before the Lord; for she thought he had forgotten her. In her time before the Lord, she cried out from her spirit; for she knew she was praying to an all-powerful God. She knew he was her only source of power.

In this day, it was the custom that when people prayed…they did so out loud. But not this day with Hannah, she did not make any sound. Yet, her lips moved. The priest Eli saw her and immediately thought her to be drunk. He approached her with deep disapproval. Upon further investigation, Eli saw that he was gravely mistaken. He saw Hannah's pain but more than that he saw her love, commitment and devotion to God. She shared with Eli the desires of her heart. She prayed to be able to bear one son. One son that she wanted for but a short while; then at the appointed time; she would give him back to the Lord. Eli saw her faith. He blessed her. She left Eli with an uplifted spirit.

God remembered Hannah for she bore a son and named him Samuel. She rejoiced for God had heard her cry and answered her prayer. She loved and care for him. As promised, at the appointed time, she took her sacrificial gifts and Samuel back to the temple of Shiloh. She worshiped the Lord there and left Samuel with Eli the priest. She kept her word to God for he had blessed her indeed. Verses 27 & 28 read "...I prayed for this child, and the Lord has granted me what I asked of him. So now I give him to the Lord. For his whole life he will be given over to the Lord." Praise God. Know that God hears you when you call on him. Know that he may not come when you want him but he's never late. He is an on-time God. We must know that God is faithful. As we walk according to his will and his way, he will bless us with the desires of our heart; for his desires and our desires become one. There is no greater experience than that of being one with God. Try God. He is the same today as he was yesterday. Know that he hears you when you call.

Hannah had developed her own personal relationship with God. She knew him to be almighty and powerful. She knew that as she cried out to him; he would hear her. She trusted God and worshipped him in spirit and in truth. She was also very humble and faithful to him. She meant all that she said to him. In this laid her blessing, for after that, she bore more children. She was blessed.

God is waiting to do the same for us today, if we only believe. Be blessed in the Lord.

Gavis Mosley

# A CHANGE HAS COME!

I recently had an opportunity to grow in faith, in what God says about me and to be a witness of who I am in Christ with an old acquaintance. We shared greetings. I was then lavished with many compliments. It was obvious that as I shared, his ears were not in tune to my voice nor his mind on my words. This person's motives were not for my good. All those kind words were just a snare, a trap to set me up to participate in old behavior. I was a bit taken back but was ever so proud to announce that not only did I look better on the outside but that my outer appearance was due to my inner change. I followed by acknowledging that God had blessed me to be the new person I am today. I no longer lived by the old way. It hurt for just a moment that this person did not see the God in me.

As I walked away, my frown turned into a smile. I knew that this would be but one of many appeals. I smiled for the Holy Spirit spoke that I would need to pray and be ready, for the enemy leaves for just a season.

2 Corinthians 5:17 says "If any man be in Christ, he is a new creature; old things are passed away; behold all things become

new". I was living this scripture. I no longer desired the things of old. The thought of such was not anything I wanted to be a part of. The reality of it all was that God had blessed me once again to be confronted with a desire of my past and I not turn my back on him. I then came to grips with my emotions; I was insulted yet grateful all in the same breath.

As I journey the word of God reigns true. I must defend the word with all my heart, mind and soul for it is truly all I can depend on. On last week, my pastor spoke about Paul and the change that God made in his life. His reference scripture was Acts 26. As I set aside time to meditate on this scripture, I was called to remember Paul and his zeal for the Lord. Go with me…

Paul is being challenged once again about his hope in Christ. He is now in prison for his teachings about Jesus. He is attempting to justify his faith and belief in Jesus as his risen Savior. Paul is boldly proclaiming the life, suffering and resurrection of Christ. He is calling King Agrippa to remember the words of the prophets. He knew that King Agrippa knew that they had been taught of a Savior who would suffer, die and be raised from the dead. Paul had preached this message to the Jews and Gentiles alike. They were all careful to remember the words of the prophet but they rejected Jesus as the Savior. They questioned how this could be the Jesus of Nazareth. Paul asked them in essence "Why not? Was there anything too hard for God?"

Paul then shared with them his life changing experience on the road to Damascus. While he was yet persecuting Christians, he was arrested by the Spirit of God. Jesus came before him as a bright blinding light. He confronted him; then, he commissioned him. Paul's heart was changed. He was now called to serve God according to his encounter. Amid doing what he thought to be right at the time, Paul was convicted by the very presence of God. He was called to be a minister of the gospel, to teach repentance and salvation to all nations. He was also called to use his encounter, his personal experience as a living testimony that Christ lives. Although he was in chains, Paul was now a free man in Christ.

On this journey, as I have been so recently reminded there will be those who will continue to see us in an old way. It is our duty to live righteous before them until God touches their life as he has touched us. It is only by the grace and mercy of God that we will continue to walk away from things of old. We must not allow anything or anyone stop us from speaking that which God has placed in our hearts concerning him. Just as Paul, we must be happy to speak boldly, with confidence of the Savior who lives. We must further acknowledge that his name is Jesus. There is power in the name of Jesus. At the sound of his name, every knee will bow and every tongue will confess that he is Lord. Knowing Jesus is knowing that your change has come.

# A MEANS TO PRAISE

I've had some good days and I've had some not so good days, but through it all, I am learning to not complain.

My grandmother has a greeting on her phone that begins " Every day is a day of thanksgiving...God is a good God." It was just days ago, that I was experiencing a not so good day. I had some things going on and I was being called to press my way through. In the midst of the day, I recalled her greeting. I instantly began to thank the Holy Spirit for delivering me from what could have been a day of anguish into one where I could still see the goodness of God and be thankful. I didn't feel well physically at all; yet, I was being called to maintain accountability. There came a point when I felt like just saying, I'm going to shut this thing down and go home. But that would not have been the best thing to do; for you see, God has just blessed me with a new job. As well, I had other commitments to attend later. People were depending on me, and I felt like…this is not my day. By this time, I was convinced that the right thing to do was to leave and just give the circumstances of that decision to God. As I contemplated further, the Holy Spirit quickened that greeting in my inner most. Every day is a day of thanksgiving. Was I determining the goodness of my day by how I felt? Was I falling prey to the "It's all about me" mentality? I was standing in a blessing, one I had prayed for and sought after, one in which I had waited patiently on the Lord to deliver; yet, I was prepared to let go of that which God had blessed me.

"Oh, No!" rose up strong in my inner man. My thoughts, my mediation changed from how I felt and how I could escape to what I could do to make it better. I knew that in and of myself, I was doomed. I immediately began to thank God for this day. I began to praise him for answering my prayers. I began to tell him just how I was feeling (as if he didn't already know) and how I needed him to help me make it through the day, to meet the obligations that he had prepared me for. I then began to think about Job.

Oh, it's good to have a word in you, to stand on in times such as this. I reflected on a recent lesson where Job was subject to the attacks which God allowed on his life. He suffered greatly physically, mentally, financially and emotionally, yet, his spirit did not waiver. He lost his children and all his worldly possessions. His wife began to speak against God, whom he loved and trusted. She asked that he curse God so that he may die. If that wasn't bad enough his so-called friends came to visit. That which was meant to be a period of consolation, turned out to be a platform for accusations. And if this wasn't enough, Job felt disconnected from God. Job was at the point of break, where he himself, willed to die. Job began to question his own faithfulness and righteousness. But Job, a true servant of God, began to recall the goodness of God and all the treasures he had found in him. Job's remembrance of his relationship with an all knowing, all powerful, all loving and merciful and peace seeking God began to strengthen him. Job declared regardless of what he was going through, that his redeemer lives. Job knew that the Lord and Master of his life would be with him, would carry him, and was able to restore him according to his will.

Oh, what a testimony of the restoring power of God. My spirit began to calm me, to lead me into asking God to just help me make it through this thing. I began to thank him for what I was going through and to speak peace and comfort to my soul. I began to speak to God confirming that it would be his strength and not mine that would carry me through this day. I asked him to increase as I decrease. I knew that it would be my faith that would carry me. I knew that God and only God would be able to keep my mind focused on all that lay before me. I asked God to increase my faith so that I would not doubt my being able to walk through this day without complaining. I stopped asking him to hold my affliction but to just allow me to allow him to carry me.

Today, I thank him. Even the more; I realize that our redeemer lives, for he lives in us. We must be aware that often we complain when we should be praising. His word tells us that all things work together for the good of those who love him. And true to his word, it has.

Today is a better day. The comforts and discomforts of our day do not determine the goodness of God. God is good all the time. Our road of circumstance is but a means to our praise. We are already blessed in the Lord.

Gavis Mosley

# A PLEA FOR THE RIGHTEOUS

Suffer it to be so that the scriptures may be fulfilled! Suffer it! Suffer it! Lord, have mercy that your purpose for my life may be fulfilled. My time has come; Lord, that I too must die to myself and live the new life in you. As you wash me in the blood of thy holy Lamb, I thank you Lord for the cleansing, for your making me whole. Lord God, I love you more than anything. I thank you for the revelation of the blood of Jesus, how it saved my soul, how it keeps me protected from dangers seen and unseen, how it keeps me in a state of praise and worship, how it allows me to stand and let you see me through, how it keeps me sure, how it wakes me in the morning, how it allows me to slumber during the night, how it ministers to my soul, how it keeps me and lets me know that you care, how it leads me and shelters me from going back to a life of dread and sin. It is in the blood that I live and it is in the blood that I shall die. For my faith lies in the blood and it's all consuming power.

What are you as a child of God asking for today? Are we more concerned with gain in our personal lives than we are the souls of our fellow sisters and brothers? For what will it profit you if you gain the whole world yet lose your soul? Do we no longer care for those who suffer around us? I declare to you, it is better that we look more closely for the one who may be lost than at the 99 we have found. We are our brother's keeper.

As children of God we are called to save lives one by one. We are called to lay petition before the Lord to have mercy on the ones who still suffer until they receive the word of God. We are called to be ambassadors of Christ. We are called to live holy and righteous before a dying world. And in our living, it is our duty to reach back and try to bring one who may be dying in a world of sin into the glorious life of living for Christ.

Go with me to Genesis 18: 26-33. Here in the scripture I see Abraham, a man of faith, a lover of mankind being his brother's keeper. God has established his covenant with Abraham. Three visitors come to the home of Abraham. Upon the conclusion of the visit, the scripture tells me that two of the visitors go ahead but God stays behind to talk to his friend. God and Abraham began to walk along the path and they looked down on the cities of Sodom and Gomorrah. When he looked down he saw sin running rampart. He saw destruction and the decline of mankind right before his eyes. There was an outcry, a bad report on the city (a great one.)

You see the Lord had blessed Abraham and his desire was to keep him safe, to keep him and his household in his will and way. With this the Lord knew the danger of being in the presence of ungodliness and unrighteousness. God knew the limitations of man. God knew the lure of temptation to the flesh of man; even its possible effect on his friend, Abraham. The Lord had decided that he would destroy the cities but he pondered on the thought of telling Abraham. Knowing Abraham's heart, the Lord shared his plan with him.

"Wow! I've got family there. Oh my, but would you destroy my folks too? But you promised life. And by the way the whole place can't be that bad, can it? There's got to be some righteous among them, there's got to be. Will you destroy the righteous with the unrighteous: Oh, surely I must make a plea for my people"? Thus, speaks the mind and heart of Abraham for he desires to be his brother's keeper.

Note: When God calls us to righteous living that is just what he means. He loves us too much to have us just wondering as if we don't know what we should be doing or how we should be living our lives. Jesus died that we may live. We have no excuse for God is calling us to be holy and righteous before him. We don't need anyone else to go to God for us. We can enter his presence one by one and make our request known to him for ourselves and for others. And by the blood of Jesus, the work on the cross, he will, I say, he will hear your cry! Now, let's journey along to the cry of Abraham…as he speaks to God.

Abraham's heart begins to question the work of God. Abraham questions if God would destroy the righteous with the wicked. Abraham said of God, "Far be it from you! Will not the Judge of all the earth do, right?" He appealed to the character of God. Abraham asked if he would save the city if there were fifty righteous to be found. The Lord says, "If I find fifty righteous people in the city of Sodom, I will spare the whole place for their sake." As the scripture reads, Abraham knew the Lord; and he begins to talk to him more closely; for his heart was still unsettled for his love for mankind was being challenged and refined. What could or should he do to petition for the life of the righteous?

He goes again before God and asked the Lord if only 20 were there would he save the city. Each time he spoke to God he did so with a sincere heart for mankind. He went from a request to a plea for the life of the righteous. As the word tells us; Lot and his family were led out and the cities were destroyed due to wickedness.

God had the authority to wipe out the cities; Abraham has the wisdom and love to appeal to the character of a righteous God. God had the power to do what he desired; Abraham had the prayer, the plea to appeal to that power for understanding. In all that we ask of God, we must know that he will always do what's right. In his right doing, the child of God will be led out before his wrath falls. The grace and mercy of God is unfailing. Had there been one righteous in the city, it is MY belief that God would have saved the city. It takes but One to save.

Judgment is the Lord's. It is the nature of God to do what is right in all circumstances. Men beware, for you carry prejudice, mistrust and fear. In considering others, seek God. We cannot always easily determine what is right and what is wrong; but rest assured that God can. He is a holy and righteous God.

Are you truly to be your brother's keeper? In our feeble being, who truly are we? I say to you; yes, you are the keeper of your brother. (Hallelujah) Be the one who cares. Be the one who shares. Someone needs to see a new way of life today…God has called us and is calling us to be the one.

What are you asking God for today? Make your request known to God according to his perfect will for you. Be blessed.

# A PRAYER OF THANKS

I am inspired today for I have had the awesome opportunity of seeing the evidence of an almighty God. On last evening, I went for a walk and upon my return, I sat outside to relax. As I was sitting there, I began to notice the calm of the evening, the low hum of traffic passing by, the sometimes quiet and sometimes not so quiet "chirps and cheeps" of whatever that was making noise in the grass, the gentle flight of a bird (must be late getting in), the color of the tree leaves are beautiful as they change from green, to brown, to orange to whatever color nature has set, then I see the tenderness, the preciousness of life – a baby rabbit hops across the lawn. It was at that moment that I began to tear up- I began to thank God- for keeping me alive. What a wonderful gift to experience – Mother Nature and Father Time.

Lord, I just want to thank you today for keeping me alive. I know Father that you are an all-consuming fire, even as I served the enemy, you stayed by my side, as my closest friend; you kept me alive. Lord, for that care, I say "Thank You." I do realize that things have not always been as well as they are, yet you were faithful to me and saw me through it all. Lord, when I was down and didn't know which way to go, you were patient and didn't give up on me, by your love and grace; you kept me alive.

God, I thank you for the "seed" that you have planted in me. I thank you for the new soil and fresh rain water that you have poured over and in me to allow that "seed" to grow. I thank you for the loving pruning you have done (and continue to do) on my branches, to keep me in place and presentable for your service. Then Lord, I thank you for the continued nourishment I get from your word; it keeps me alive.

Lord, I thank you for being the wind beneath my wings. There were many times along the way that I've felt like giving up- folding in but Father you would not let me. You let me know that I must continue, to win. I know that I have acted like a "baby birdie" fresh out of the egg at times. (Chirp, chirp). I was wet and afraid. I would venture to the edge of a breakthrough in my faith and be too afraid "to try" to flap my wings; spread my wings as you had directed. Instead, I would scamper back into my comfort zone and "let it be". But today God, I thank you that you never "let me be." You kept after me; you wanted the best for me. You knew all that you had made me to be and you did not let go. When others said I could not, you said, yes you can and yes you will. I am so grateful for you being there, the day I trusted your word enough to step out of all the "mess in the nest"; go to the edge; and take my leap of faith. I could spread my wings. When I was unstable in my flight, you provided just enough air support to keep me airborne. You never let me fall. When I became tired, you strengthened me. When I became weary, you encouraged me. When I wanted to just throw in the towel, (go back to the nest, my comfort zone), you loved me.

As I journey in my faith, my trust, and my walk with you, I thank you. I thank you. I thank you for now I can soar like an eagle, wings spread wide, bold in full flight, head up facing the heavens, looking unto you, my source of life. You are the wind beneath my wings. God, I thank you for this flight! Today I soar in the glory and in the power of your strength and your might. It has truly been amazing to see you, to be close to you as you have continued to mold me and shape me. From the weak, shaky, little wet birdie to a beautiful soaring bold eagle – You have kept me alive!

What he has done for me, he will do it for you. He is our keeper, our help, our refuge. Amen.

Gavis Mosley

# A TOUCH

It's deep. It's piercing. It's everlasting. It's love, mercy and grace all wrapped tight, bound together. It's penetrating beneath the skin and bones, it goes straight to the heart, the nucleus, the center of life itself, where it all begins. It is a touch from the Lord. It's life changing, mind regulating and spirit defining.

In all that we do, we need the Lord. He is the true source of our strength. His word, his promises gives us the assurance and relief we need to carry on in times when we just don't know, in and of ourselves, what to do. It is then that we must gather our being and call on the name of the Lord, for he cares.

Our first life experiences were centered around being touched. From infancy throughout childhood our most precious remembrances lie in a touch...whether it be physical or emotional. As a child, we remember the gentleness, the comfort, and the assurance that we found in the touch of a loving mother. It took but just a touch of her hand or lips and regardless the problem, we were immediately healed. We trusted that touch to take the pain out of our most recent hurt; to calm our deepest fear; to protect us when we felt afraid; to comfort us during our moments of insecurity and doubt. Most of all, it was confirmation to us of an unfailing, ever present available love. For the believer and soon to be believer, what more do we have in the one true and living, all powerful and knowing God!

As we journey, we need more; Our spirit seeks for more. We begin to search for power from within. We need a touch that will sustain us internally while externally the attack keeps coming. We need something that will keep us when the pressure begins to cause us to bend, we need to hold on and not break. We need a touch from the Lord.

We need a touch that won't leave us nor forsake us; we need it to be faithful and wonderful. We need one that will never lose its power; from one that has all power in the palm of his hand over the heavens and earth. We need a touch that can be found everywhere and at any time. I'm speaking of a touch…a touch from God.

Now this would be the same touch that delivered Shadrach, Meshach and Abednego from the fiery furnace. It is the touch that healed the woman who had suffered for years with the issue of blood. The touch was the provider as Abraham and Issacs went up to worship. It is the one that grants favor to the just as well as the unjust. The touch protected as Ester went before the king to save her nation. That same touch brought comfort to Mary as she pondered, thought in her heart about giving birth to the Savior of the world. He counseled Daniel and gave him wisdom to interpret dreams and visions. He delighted David so much that he danced. It is that same touch that quickens in my soul today as I think on the goodness of the Lord. I'm still speaking of a touch.

It strengthens when we are weak; it encourages when we are in doubt. It leads us and guides us on this path as we uplift and glorify the kingdom. It is the very air that we breathe. It is our shelter from the pride of feeling self-empowered and from being greedy in success. As well, it is our shelter, our refuge in the storms of life. A touch…from the Lord…means everything. Even though it comes with love, mercy and grace; it can also come with wrath when correction and growth is needed. It lifts us up when we have fallen as well as brings us down when we have gotten too high and mighty. It is prefect in making a dark situation bright.

Just one touch from God can be your shelter for life if you only believe. We must keep the faith and believe in Jesus as our Lord and Savior. It will be then and only then that we will be able to experience the joy, I say the unspeakable joy, the overflowing joy of the touch. It redeems, it is precious and strong; genuine and true. It is loving and correcting as we move to a higher purpose and place in the Lord.

I'm speaking of a touch…not just any touch…but a touch from the Lord.

Gavis Mosley

# ACCEPT WHAT GOD ALLOWS

"Taste and see that the Lord is good; blessed is the man who takes refuge in him. Fear the Lord, you his saints, for those who fear him lack nothing. The lions may grow weak and hungry, but those who seek the Lord lack no good thing." As we journey and taste of God, we must accept what God allows.

Lord, I thank you for your goodness and your mercy. I thank you for being my beginning and my end. I thank you for your all-consuming fire. I thank you, Lord, for having removed me from the low shelf of life and now you have made me a treasure fit for the pedestal. Father, God, I love you more than anything. Lord, I thank you for breaking chains in my life. Lord, the strongholds that used to bind me can no longer find me; for I now rest in the shadow of the Almighty. Lord, often, I can hear the chains of my past attempting to speak to my present; but, I also hear your command to those chains. "Peace. Be Still." In the twinkling of an eye, I am released from the mere presence of all danger. Lord, I thank you that you have brought all things under your authority. Lord Almighty, I thank you for your goodness and your righteousness. Lord, help me to allow you to have your way in my life today.

Accepting what God allows can be a trying experience. But, the reward is often much greater than you would ever imagine.
As I journey, accepting what God allows requires faith and trust in God, who he is and all that he must say. It requires staying committed to his word despite all the chaos that may be going on around me. It requires staying faithful when all seem to have lost faith and hope in me. It requires holding on when there is little or nothing to hold on to. It requires falling on my knees time and time again and knowing that I must wait on the Lord. It requires marching on in the army of the Lord while my toes are constantly being stumped in battle. It includes being taken advantage of and being able to not retaliate. It requires turning the other cheek. (Lord have mercy.)

When we accept what God allows…we humble ourselves in the Lord. He will exalt us. When we have been obedient and have done all God has called us to do and confusion still comes…we must accept what God allows.

Please journey with me to Genesis Chapter 12 and 13. In Chapter 12, God blessed Abram with a promise for he walked in faith. He commands Abram to leave his country, his people and his father's household to go to a land that he would show him. (Give up all and go where?) Out of obedience, Abram journeyed to a place of promise where "I will make you into a great nation and I will bless you; I will make your name great and you will be a blessing. I will bless those who bless you, and whoever curses you I will curse; and all people on earth will be blessed through you." He took his nephew Lot with him. He encountered trouble along the way but he continued to journey to a place of promise. He got caught up in deceit, lies, fear and shame but he continued to journey to a place of promise. He was called on to share and be responsible for folk who did not share his faith and commitment yet he continued to journey to a place of promise. He was faced with trials and tribulations yet he journeyed. Through it all, he trusted and believed in God.

By the time Abram arrived at Bethel, the place of promise, he and his nephew had acquired great wealth. It says in the scripture that Abram called on the name of the Lord for he was a man of worship. As Abram worshipped, conflict began to break out between the two men and their herdsman. Their possessions were so great that the land could not support both. Abram, a man of God, went to Lot to offer up (to let go) a portion of the land to him. Abram offered Lot that which had been promised to him. Abram was willing to give Lot whatever it would require restoring peace. Lot looked out and selected what appeared to him to be the choice piece of land that would be more than enough to support him. Lot selected the fertile land, the vast supply of water, the abundant camp ground. Oh Yea, thought Lot, this is it!

Abram agreed and they parted. Now Abram did not quarrel for his trust lied in God. (Know that we will never receive what God has for us unless we are willing to give up everything to get it.) From that very place of what now appeared "lack," "not enough" …look at God. Chapter 13 Verse 14 tells me that God told Abram to "Lift up your eyes from where you are and look north and south, east and west. It all belongs to you. Look up and see what I have for you."

Know that when man has taken things away, when you have been treated unjustly; if you have remained in the will of God; God will come to you and say…" Do not focus on the negative…move forward into what I have for you." God does not want conflict or strife between his people. We must come to a place where getting our way or having possessions, does not get in the way of our peace.

No matter what a person takes away or how badly they may act…do not allow it to separate you from the love, the joy, the peace of God. For if you accept what God allows…be it a disappointment, a tornado, bankruptcy, illness, death…whatever it may be…he has a promise for you…" I will make you into a great nation and I will bless you." Don't question God; he is worthy of our faith, our trust; he is the only Hope. Accept what God allows. Be blessed in the Lord.

# AND DAVID DANCED

There comes a time and a place when nothing else matters but being in the presence of Jehovah God. There's a hope for a better, brighter and stronger future for the believer. Let us rejoice in the hope of the day when we do not act out of what comes natural to us but out of our God consciousness. There's a hope that we will allow the spirit of God to consume us and then and only then will we be able to understand and appreciate the dance.

God is calling us to build our hope on those things that are eternal. We can have the eternal hope. All we must do is believe in the work that Christ did for us on the cross. We must believe the work to be complete and that it was for us because he loved us just that much. We must believe in Jesus and the power of the word of God. We must believe God to be all knowing and all powerful. We must believe that God is everywhere and that he reigns. Most importantly, we must believe that God is near and that he cares. Trusting God is the foundation on which we should build our faith for he is perfect in his faithfulness to us. Even in times of judgement, he reminds us, he encourages us for he tells us that we will be forgiven, and restored back to him if only we repent and worship him and him alone for he is a jealous God.

Know that God is good and that he will not fail. Know that the Lord our God sits high but he looks low. He sees us every day all day long. We are never alone. God knows everything about us. He knows our thoughts before we even think them. He knows what we will do and what we will not do. He knows. He is our creator. If we think he doesn't know then think again; we are only fooling ourselves. He is the protector from dangers seen and unseen. He desires that we would just spend time with him. Since he already knows us, we need to get to know him. This can only be done by spending one on one-time, personal, special time with him. We need to spend time reading the word of God, praying to him (talking to him) and mediating on his word day and night (think on those things that we read and ask God to help us to understand what it is that he wants us to get out of it and how we should apply it to our lives).

It is in our trusting God that we will praise and we will worship him. It is through our knowledge of God that our lives are transformed; our minds are renewed; our walk becomes clear and our talk is more productive. God desires to use that which he has put in us for his purpose. In God, is where our faith and trust should begin and end. He is the keeper of his promises, he is the healer of all our hurts, he is the comforter when we have been shaken and he is the refuge for the broken hearted. God is near all the time.

He desires that we fortify ourselves in him. He wants to meet us in our secret place. Our secret place…a place of caring, sharing, giving and receiving. It is a place of refuge where we cast all our cares on him, it is a place of praise where we show him just how thankful/grateful we are for all things. It is a place where when the weight of the world seems too heavy God himself will carry that heavy load for us. It is a place where the storm may be raging but we will only see the rainbow. It is a place of worship where we acknowledge God for his being God. It is a place where we realize the teachings and revelation of God to be true. It is that quiet, calm place where we are one with God the Father, Jesus our Savior, and the Holy Spirit. It is in this place that the promises of God are renewed in our spirit, where our hope in the eternal is once again realized. It is here that the power and awesomeness of love come alive. It is here that our thoughts and plans are surrendered unto the will of God. It is here where our focus changes from the affairs of the world to the creator of life. The preciousness of just another day of grace and mercy becomes a song in our heart…it is in this place that we will dance.

As we dance, we find hope and assurance in the presence of God. We come to accept the trials and tribulations of life as stepping stones to be cherished not dreaded. It is through our trials that we become refined work of the potter. It is in the potter's hands that we are broken, molded, reshaped, flattened and then pressed so that fresh oil flows both on us and through us. Broken pieces are re-established, restored, refined. We are made brand new in the presence of God. It is the place where every knee will bow and every tongue will confess that Jesus is Lord. It is in this place that the issues of the heart flow out of our mouths into the hands of God. Thus, as we dance, we will experience the joy of the Lord. When we experience the joy of the Lord, his spirit radiates in our mannerisms, our speech, and our presentation. Where the spirit of the Lord is there is liberty. We are no longer held in bondage.

I'm reminded of David as he danced before the Lord. King David, former shepherd boy, giant slayer, mighty warrior, adulterer, accomplice to murder, the one who ran from cave to cave, city to city from Saul, the one whose life span witnessed episodes ranging from misery to ministry…Yea that David. David wore many titles in his life (just as you and I have). but the one that reigns today is man after the heart of God. (Come what may know that God is a transformer of life.) I'm reminded of King David as he celebrated God.

2 Samuel 6:14 says "Wearing a linen ephod, David was dancing before the Lord with all his might." And David danced. First, in this day, men normally did not dance. Secondly, especially the king did not dance (in public anyway.) They were spectators of the women celebrating, dancing in the streets; but the scripture tells me that King David danced. He danced not in his kingly attire but in the essentials. Oh, what a dance! David set aside all that mattered in the physical (material things) so that he could fully celebrate the joy he felt in his heart. For you see, a lifelong desire was being realized, goodness and favor were on David for he couldn't help it, he danced. David danced in expression of joy and thankfulness of all that the Lord meant to him. The word tells me that he danced with all his might. This tells me that David had a move of his own, jumping and leaping all over the place out of an inner excitement that could not be contained. Dancing in celebration of the Ark of God (symbolic of the very presence of

God) being brought into the city of David. With all that came with bringing the Ark to the city and what it symbolized…the oppression of the children of God…the ark had been left just sitting unaccounted for, for years…the death of Uzziah who with good intentions had touched the Ark to keep it from falling…down to being a disgrace to his wife…David danced. He celebrated in spite of. We too are called to celebrate God. Come what may, nothing else should matter, when we celebrate God. God is worthy. God is wonderful.

We have the word of God and his promises that gives us the assurance of our victory in Christ. Romans 8:28 says "And we know that in all things God works for the good of those who love him, who have been called according to this purpose." We are the called.

He has equipped us for this journey. We are called to obey and trust God for he is faithful. Pray for wisdom and understanding. Be grateful for each day and as you grow in the word, God will grow in you. If God is for you, who can be against you. For greater is he who is in you than he who is in the world. The spirit of the Lord is in this place. I ask you "Who is like the Lord?"

Come what may, as you meditate on the word, consider life, eternal life with the Lord. We are more than conquerors as we move in the power of the Lord. Let the people of God give all praise to him. Let all the generations come together and celebrate his goodness. We are called to magnify the Lord. And yes, we are called to dance and celebrate the Lord. How? you may ask…just dance…like David danced! You are already blessed in the Lord.

Gavis Mosley

# AND JUST WHO ARE YOU

As I journey, it has been revealed to me that I must remain steadfast and unmovable in the word of God. With that, I must always be teachable. I should guard against a spirit of judgment and prejudice. I must guard against looking at the messenger and thereby missing the message for there is a blessing in every message from God. I have come to realize that God can and will use whomever he chooses to build his kingdom, to be his witness and to give him glory. He has taken my test and turned it into my testimony. He has cleaned up my mess; so that today, I have a message to share. Oh, I know he will do it. Who would have thought, he's using me! Won't he do it!

I thank God that there are no little I's and big U's in his Kingdom and that all have fallen short of his glory, therefore, we have no room to talk about each other. We have no right to judge or to discriminate because the word of God says that the penalty to us all is DEATH.

We, as children of God, are called to receive the message (the word of God) and are not called to judge the messenger. We do have the responsibility to lay that message next to the word of God to verify its truth. It must line up. I am once again amazed; as I too, have had a change in perspective. I had consciously decided there were speakers/preachers that I could listen to, and there were some that I could not base solely on my unforgiving thoughts, my limited understanding, and yes, my prejudice. But God, then called me to be teachable. Before I can discriminate I must first educate (myself that is) to the word of God. I must know the truth for myself and thereby I would be able to receive his uncompromised word from those whom he sends my way to share the gospel of Jesus Christ. It was at a time in my journey that I was asking God for more of him. He called me then to study and show myself approved and to know his voice. He taught me to listen with the spirit that he had given me and to stop looking at the flesh of man. For I was doing that which had been done to me, I was judging another based on their performance and not receiving by the word of God. Forgive me, Lord.

Forgive me, Lord, for my "not so teachable moments". I know that you can use anyone and anything for your glory. I know that you did not start or stop saving folk when you saved me. I ask that you will close my ears to the gossip of and about man and open my heart to your word regardless of the source; so that I will not miss that which you have for me. I know that it is your will that must be done so that your Kingdom will come.

I am taken to 2 Kings Chapter 5. For this I know; faith comes from hearing the message, and the message is heard through the word of Christ. It tells of a prominent man being able to receive a message of God from a servant. God can and will use anyone to further his Kingdom, to save lives and to bring all those he calls unto him.

It tells of Naaman, a great man in the sight of the king of Aram, a mighty warrior who had been victorious in battle, but he had leprosy. (Leprosy in this day was not good; people were outcast and separated from the general population.) It so happens that on one of the outings that the army captured a slave girl from Israel. Oh, she was a committed, faithful, and smart one. (She like Daniel was taken from her homeland but she took her God and her faith in him with her. She had the word hidden in her heart. She took advantage of an opportunity to share her God with someone, Oh what a witness.) The slave girl was a servant to Naaman's wife and she told his wife that she knew of a prophet, a man of God in Israel, who could heal Naaman. The wife believed and spoke to Naaman who was later granted permission to travel to seek out the prophet. When he arrived at Elisha's door, Elisha sent a servant out to give him his instructions regarding what to do to be healed. Go to the Jordan River and wash yourself seven times and your flesh will be clean. Well, there was nothing profound about that. He could have gone to any more elaborate, cleaner river in his own land and washed; if this was it. Oh no. He needed, or felt he did anyway, a "whoopla"; where were the bells and whistles? Oh, Naaman's expectations were much higher for a healing; he refused the word, became angry and began to walk away. (We must be careful with our perceived ideas about people and how God works for we just may be positioning ourselves to miss our blessing. He doubted the validity of the man of God.)

As the servants urged Naaman to be obedient to the word of Elisha, his anger softened. He was persuaded to go the Jordan.

Sure enough, he washed himself as instructed and he was restored. All Praises to God. Glory to God in the highest. Hallelujah. Joy and Unspeakable Joy. Blessings and Glory. Naaman and his servants returned to bear gifts and to thank Elisha. Now when Naaman returned, he stood before Elisha, humble and healed. He acknowledged God as the God of the world (his God) and offered gifts to Elisha. In keeping with his faith, Elisha would not receive the gifts for all his help came from God. He didn't want to receive the praise for he knew it all belonged to God. Having been able to play a role in opening Naaman's eyes was his reward.

It was by receiving the message from an unfamiliar and unlikely messenger that Naaman was healed. I want you to know today that we are all that servant girl. We are called to spread the Gospel of Jesus Christ. We are called to go forth into a dying world and give new life. We are to speak boldly and openly of the things we know of the Lord. By that same token, we are called to not discriminate against one who may be sent to teach us. Look beyond the packaging, open it up and check out what's inside. Do you see any attribute of God and do you hear his word?

For this I know, I, myself am just one, trying to tell everybody, about somebody who can save anybody! Be blessed in the Lord.

# ANGELS WATCHING OVER ME

As my spirit speaks; Lord, I thank you for the angels that are watching over me. I can feel them Lord all about me. I hear them ministering to me at this very moment. I know that they are there. They are speaking peace to my storm. They are speaking calm to the war that was trying to rage within me. They are speaking victory as the enemy attacks from all sides. They are speaking healing to the demons of sickness. They are speaking deliverance from those things that continue to try to hinder me. They are speaking joy to my soul in a time in my life when I am experiencing doubt. They are speaking comfort where there was once turmoil. They are speaking truth where there was once only lies and deceit. They are speaking faith where there is disbelief. They are speaking encouragement where there was once defeat. Oh, speak to me Lord as your/my angels watch over me! In my humble state Lord, I see you speaking prosperity, and I thank you in advance for what you are doing. Lord, I find power and authority in your presence. Oh, I tell you the truth, I would not take anything for my journey right now. Neither silver nor gold, for Jesus lives today, he lives in my soul. By the power and authority of Jesus, angels watch over me all night and all day!

As I journey, I am called into obedience, submission and transformation. I am called to keep moving, to keep growing and to be about the business which has been placed before me. I know that the spiritual atmosphere is powerful

I recently got news of misbehavior. Oh yea, bad girl. Bad Girl! As I listened to what was going on in my child's life, my immediate reaction was one of guilt, sadness and blame. If I had been there, then I could have done this or that. (What about the power of God covers and transcends any mile that man may have between them.) If I had not been such an irresponsible person myself then… (now am I ready to change my testimony on how God blessed me through this trial and how he has turned my life around.)

Oh Lord, how do I speak to her on these issues when she is a product of what I have laid before her. (I should speak to her by the power and authority of new life that God has placed in me. I no longer walk in darkness and it is now time to share the new life with her…but can I?) Oh, for all of 15 minutes I labored on what to do. I was being bullied by a report from the enemy. I, for a moment, was listening to a voice from my old way of life that was causing me to fear and doubt those things that God had told me were behind me. The enemy was coming once again and attacking someone dear to me and I felt like running and hiding in the excuses of my past failures, disappointments and guilt.

I was quickly reminded of the prophet Elisha in 1 Kings 19. He was called by the Lord to speak to his disobedient nation. He looked at what was before him, then at who was sending him. He trusted God. He went forth in the power and authority of God. He allowed God to go before him to claim the victory. He made a plea for the people as well as the false prophets of Baal and Asherah to meet him at Mount Carmel. It was there that he questioned the people as to whom they would serve. He challenged them to heed what was before them. He then put the idols to test. He needed to prove to the people that there was only one true and living God. Each test that he put before the idols...they failed. They were a disgrace before the people. He then called the people to seize the false prophets of Baal and Asherah to be slaughtered. All this he did in the power, authority and might of God.

Immediately after this, he got word not from King Ahab but from his wife, Jezebel, that she wanted him dead. Before he could find himself...he took off to the hills, running just as fast as he could from a threat of the enemy. I see a prophet, a man of God, a mighty deliverer of the word, one victorious in battle, turn tail and run because he has been threatened by the enemy. Oh, mighty man of God where is your faith as you run; where is your trust that you proclaimed just yesterday; where is that man of valor who is called to stand on the word of God? Where is he? Where is he? I'll tell you where he is...he's running, he's running scared for his very life; a life that belongs to God. Once he got to his haven, he came to a still quiet place where he could rest. He came to a place where the forces from the outside could no longer distract him. He returned to a place where he could see God. It was in this place of fear, doubt and unbelief that he came face to face with his Father who is mighty in battle. It was in his place of defeat that he found victory, joy, power and authority over the enemy.

As I reminisce on this bible truth, I ask was he running from the enemy or was he running to God? I choose to believe a little of both. For the word of the enemy caused him to go to where he could hear from God; to a place of restoration, of regeneration, of renewal.

On this given day, I too was being given a report from the enemy and I had the urge to run and hide; but God said different. He reminded me of how far he had brought me to prepare me for such a time as this. He reminded me that I say daily that I trust him (well). He reminded me that it is he who is supplying the very air that I breathe (what could I be thinking.) What could possibly be so great as to fear the voice of the enemy? Ultimately so profoundly, he so clearly spoke, I am restoring your years, your years of "no show", your years of "lies", your years of "guilt and shame," your years of "misuse and abuse". I'm restoring you.

Oh Yea! I thank you Lord. It was then and only then that I able to call my daughter and minister to her from the word of God boldly and with assurance. God allowed me to speak to her with love, peace and acceptance. God allowed me to witness to her, to be a light in a dark moment; to be a message of love and acceptance, to be a message of assurance in her time of confusion. God allowed me today to do and to be that what I could not do on yesterday…be a Mother! And for that, I say Thank You. For God is restoring me, he's restoring me, he's restoring me. He's taking me to a special place in him where I can be all that he has called me to be.

As I journey, as I face the trials of life, I pray that I will know that not only is God watching over me, he dispatches angels to me in my times of trouble. For it is this truth, on this given day, that kept me from a spirit of "flight" but brought me to one of "might". As for my child, she too must learn to listen to the still quiet voice of God. She too must learn to trust and believe God. She too must know of him for herself. She too must surrender the old way of life to a new life that can only be found in Jesus Christ. She too must experience her angels watching over her.

Father God, I thank you for once again showing yourself to be true. I pray that we grow in the Lord and continue to experience his power and authority over the enemy. I pray my strength and your strength in the Lord. For this I know, I have angels watching over me. With that, I want you to know, you have angels watching over you.

Be blessed in the Lord.

Gavis Mosley

# ASK GOD

Ask God to do it for you. He can change you. Forgiveness is but a confession away. You can never go where he can't reach you. You can never speak so low that he will not hear you. "He who cover his sins will not prosper, but whoever confesses and forsakes them will have mercy." As I journey, I ask that God would speak to my heart.

Today has been a good day. It has been a great day and all praises to God. I find myself in the company of believers and testimonies to the goodness and majesty of God.

A co-worker whom I choose to refer to as Baby Bear shared a word dear to her heart with me. It was Psalms 32:7. "You are my hiding place, you will protect me from trouble and surround me with songs of deliverance." As she shared, my spirit quickened. "It is written," Romans 14:11 "As surely as I live, says the Lord, 'every knee will bow before me; every tongue will acknowledge God."

I immediately meditated on the thought that we are so blessed to know the Lord in the pardoning, the forgiveness of our sins. We are blessed to have, to serve a God who loves us unconditionally.

We are blessed to have a God who created us in his image. We are blessed to have a God who gave up his only Son so that we may have life in him. We are blessed because above all things, we have been forgiven.

Often, we agonize over the process of being forgiven for we first must confess. Confession is a personal matter. No one can do it for you. Only you and God know what you have done and the person or persons you may have done it with. But it will be you and God who will settle your record, not you and someone else. Often the feelings of guilt, shame, jealousy, envy and many others will serve to hinder the process; but when God says enough is enough, then you must bear all before him. Oh, what a healing process it is. But first you must know that you were not the first to have to go before the Lord for forgiveness and you won't be the last. The word of God encourages us to seek him while he can be found.

I am taken to a song that says that it's good to know Jesus, it's good to know the Lord; so true, so true. Where would I be if it had not been for the Lord on my side? Oh, where would I be? The answer to that question is the foundation of my faith. For without the Lord whom I call God I would be a wrecked canoe floating aimlessly in a mighty body of water without a paddle or compass. I would be a lost soul moving about without any direction or purpose. I would be easy prey for the next predator in the food chain. I would be like a single leaf having been blown from a skinny tree being tossed to and fro on a windy, cold winter night. I would be easily consumed. I would be nothing without the Lord and his love, mercy, grace and forgiveness.

For just a moment I would like for you to go with me to Psalms 32 where it speaks of one who loved the Lord dearly. He is "one who was after the very heart of God", it is David. In my remembrance, there was a time when I could only see me and that was not pretty. I was lost and as guilty as I could be. Guilty I tell you. It was God who spoke to my soul. It was Jesus who paid my sin debt so that I could have liberty. He held me, he kept me, and he cleansed me, so that I could share my testimony. It was truly the grace, mercy and love of God that I can see more today…for I am chosen, I am forgiven, I am saved and I am free.

Here we find David giving praises to God. He has received a promise from God and he is rejoicing. Prior to rejoicing, David found himself, just as I have and you too, in a state of total rebellion, denial, disobedience, cover up, guilt and shame. He says, immediately blessed is the man whose sin God has covered, forgiven. When we sin, we are burdened and heavily laden. We carry around a load in our physical body and well as our spirit that we were not designed to carry. We are designed to be holy not full of holes! We often try to dismiss or rationalize our sins but that sound mind and clean heart that God has given us won't let you rest in peace. The more you try to hide and cover up the more "it" will be revealed. (You can't hide anything from God.) David realized that after all he had done, and all he had done to cover it up, he could not hide it or himself from God. At his wits end, he lays out in total surrender and repentance. As God meets him in his hour of submission, he is restored. David can now worship God in spirit and truth. God is faithful and he is just. He does what he does because he is holy and he is God alone.

God desires that we come into and remain in his rest. During it all, God will become our "hiding place", our place of refuge, our place of serenity. For it is in God and his word where we find our protection and comfort. The word of God is our weapon. It will protect us, teach us and guide us. Our obedience to his word will be our assurance that we won't go back, turn back to those dark places. As the Lord lifts us up, he begins to instruct us in his ways and he promises to watch over us for he neither sleeps nor slumber. God's unfailing love surrounds the man who trusts in him.

I will be the first to admit that coming clean with God is a very humbling experience as well as a necessary one for every believer. It is in this process that you are cleansed by the blood of Jesus. It is in this process that you can change out of your grave clothes and put on the righteousness of God. It is in this process that you learn the importance of being forgiven thus you become forgiving. Amen lights. It is in this process that God has turned your mess into his message. It is in this process that it becomes less about you but more about him. It is in this process that you have become a part of the Master's Plan.

Allow today to be your day to come to God. Seek him with your whole heart. Seek out the treasures that are stored up just for you. There are promises with your name on them in the word of God. God had done the first works for you, he has given up Jesus for you while you were yet in your sins. If you are a believer, then stay before the Lord and know that daily we fall short, we must also confess our sins to God and ask for forgiveness. There's nothing that you and God cannot handle. God's love for us is beyond understanding. If you are ready to go higher, lift your finger and before you know it, God will be holding your hand. In Jesus name, with a sincere heart, forgiveness and new life is but a confession away. Be blessed in the Lord.

Gavis Mosley

# BE ENCOURAGED

In our own way, in the strength that God is allowing…we must proclaim…This is a day that the Lord has made …let us rejoice and be glad in it.

The scripture says let everything that has breathe praise the Lord. I've come to encourage you today. You need to know that we all have a praise in us.

It may be in your hand clap or the stomp of your foot. It may be in the move of your nose or in the wiggle of your toes. We all have a praise in us. It may be in the out pouring of words or maybe just the twinkle in your eye. We all have a praise to God within us. When we praise God we are encouraged. We are no longer thinking of ourselves and our own issues or challenges; for our focus is turned to one who is greater. For you see he is one who is mighty and strong in battle, we see one who has gone with us and been by our side down through the years; we see one who at times has carried us through danger seen and unseen. We see one who has gone before us and made a way when there was no way.

My brothers and my sisters, I've come to encourage you today, just to tell you that the best is yet to come. I challenge you to hold on to all that God is speaking into you because you haven't seen nothing yet. One day you will, we all will, put on our robe and tell the story of how we made it over. But until that day comes…be encouraged. It's not over until the Lord says it's over. Each day his grace and mercy is new in us. Daily as God blesses you to wake, in that portion of health and strength that he has given you, give him the praise. Praise God. Know that as you draw near to him he is drawing just that much closer to you. God has some promises that he's going to fulfill in your life. You are still full of promise and purpose. Look at what he did in the life of Abraham and Sarah. Man's limitations are God's opportunities. He made them a promise in their later years that in the eyes of man seemed impossible; but by the faith of God we have learned that all things are possible. He promised Abraham that he would be the father of many nations. And so it was. He promised Sarah that a once barren body would produce fruit and so it did. God has but to speak his word upon us and it is done. And since you are here today…he is speaking new life, new birth, new strength, new power, new mercy and grace into you right now.

Every day wake up knowing that God loves you, he is with you and that he has not forgotten about you. He cares for you. You are blessed with years, wisdom and life that have only been granted to you by our Father who is in heaven. His eyes are on the sparrow so you know that he is watching over you. He sits high yet he looks low for he know everything we do and everyplace we go. It's no mistake that you are here today. He has prepared you to be a testimony to his goodness, his grace and his mercy. Be encouraged because God continues to find you worth saving, worth keeping you here for yet another day. Allow God to keep cleansing you from the inside out. Look not unto your circumstance but to the God of the circumstance. Look to the one who supplies all your needs. Look to the one who speaks and it is so. Look to the one who woke you us this morning and started you on your way. Look to the one who neither sleep nor slumber. Look to the one who promises never to leave you nor forsake you. Look to the one who has prepared a place for you; for where he goes, you will be their also. Look to the one who holds you in the very palm of his hand. And when the day gets heavy and the night grows long...look to the hill from which all your help comes.

I am reminded of the widow woman who was gathering sticks preparing to die. In steps Elisha needing a bite to eat. She has nothing to give; (so she thought), for she was going to cook her last then she and her son would die. But she heard a request from the Lord, she obeyed and she not only lived but her cupboards never were empty again. In this, I say to you, we all have something to give, something to offer, for we are vessels of the Lord. In what may appear like nothing to you, you may feel limited, restrained, but not so...God can and will use you just the way you are to fulfill his word and purpose. Be encouraged. He's the same God today, trust him, and love him. Allow him to love you, care for you, comfort you, protect you and deliver you. Desire all of him and all that he has for you.

I encourage you to visit with one another whenever possible. You are not alone. God has blessed us to be here in order that we may share our journey with each other. Know that there should not be a question in your mind as to the greatness of God. He is everywhere always. I can hear the testimony of David "A man's goings are established of Jehovah; and he delights in his way. Though he falls, he shall not be cast down; for Jehovah upholds him with his hand. I have been young and now am old; yet have I not seen the righteous forsaken, nor his seed begging bread." You are the righteous, you are the called of God.

When the lights grow dim and all gets still and quiet about you, do not fear, do not be afraid, be encouraged for God is near. God desires that you hide his word in your heart so that it may bring you comfort and good cheer. His word will protect you during all difficult moments. It will console you when all else is gone. The word of God, the Holy Spirit that dwells within you are all that you need…be encouraged.

Isaiah 41:10 'Be encouraged, "so do not fear, for I am with you; do not be dismayed, for I am your God. I will strengthen you and help you; I will uphold you with my righteous right hand."
Psalms 16:8 Keep your eyes always on the Lord so that you will not be shaken. Be encouraged.

Psalms 55:22 Cast your cares on the Lord and he will sustain you; he will never let the righteous be shaken.

Psalms 119:50 My comfort in my suffering is this; Your promise preserves my life.

And Psalms 46: 1 –God is our refuse and strength, an ever-present help in trouble. Therefore, we will not fear, though the earth gives way and the mountains fall into the sea, though its waters roar and foam and the mountains quake with their surging. There is a river whose streams make glad the city of God, the holy place where the Most High dwells. God is within her, she will not fall; God will help her at break of day. Know that at our break of day…we will not fall…we are not alone…The Lord Almighty is with us; The God of Jacob is our fortress. Be Encouraged in the Lord.

Gavis Mosley

# BELIEVE GOD

We are a chosen generation ---we should bring forth the praises of God. Sometimes we find ourselves under the attack of the enemy in an unexpected way. Yet, the good news is, there is an answer because of who we are in Jesus Christ. It is time that we realize that this journey is about us also. We have a role to play in what goes on in our life. We are a chosen generation. We have been called into abundant life. In the abundant life that we have found in Jesus Christ, our past has been cast into the sea of "no more". We have been redeemed by the blood of Jesus. We must know who we are in Jesus Christ. I thank God for lifting me when I felt so weighed down. Thank you, for I am being transformed from this world.

I am reminded daily that it's me Oh Lord…I stand in the need of prayer. As I journey, I am revived each day in the name of Jesus. I must be regenerated daily by the living water that flows without end. I thank you. I have been prepared for such a time as this. I can say this because God is showing me what to do along the way! In times of adversity, Lord, I need you…less of me and more of you…is what I need. You know and I know that I am not able to stand without you. I seek you Lord to keep me lifted. Lord, it is you who enables me to walk in authority. I need to keep my mind, my heart and my ways focused on what you say about my trouble not on what I think I see. Lord, as I walk, help me to know that you are the God of the impossible. For me to be victorious, I must know beyond a shadow of a doubt that "God is able to take all things, I say all things, and work them out for my good because his word says he would." As I journey…

If I am not careful a negative situation or circumstance can and will quickly take my eyes off God. I will focus completely on the negative thing that has come to hinder me. But I must…be of good cheer and stand on the word of God. I must stand and see the salvation of God; for there, I will find my strength.

When I speak of adversity, I speak of that situation, person or obstacle that comes against me to stop my progress or work against my well-being. Job 14:1 tells me "Man is born of woman; his days are few and full of trouble." This means, from day one until the very last day, I will experience throughout life issues that touch my soul. They will come in all shapes, colors and sizes. By the word of God, they will come.

As a child of God, what am I to do? Run, hide, avoid. No. As a child of God, I am called to know God. God promises to stand with me and help me to overcome that which has come against me; for he is my help, my refuge in the time of trouble. I have a choice of believing what God says or focusing on the lie (that which Satan has brought) that I can't bear this what I now face. I am now called to believe God. In times of distress; I am called to remember, meditate on, believe and stand on the word of God. I must know that my future is not shaped by the problems I have in life but by my attitude as I face them in the will of God. I must remain under his protection, his guidance, his shelter in order that I am not consumed.

I reflect on the life of David, a man after the very heart of God. From a puny shepherd boy to a mighty man of valor to a seasoned man of God, he faced adversity. As he faced his giants, for he had many, he did so under the counselor of God. As he slung his rock into Goliath, he did so under the power of God. As he conquered nations as a mighty warrior, he did so under the authority of God. As he hid and ran from Saul, he did so in the love of God. As he proclaimed the goodness of God as a seasoned man, he did so in the wisdom of God. David knew that in the day of despair, adversity, or change he could call on God and that God would be there. David was not perfect in his walk by any means but he trusted God. He believed on the word of God. Just as God was there for David, he is there for you, he is there for me. We must believe.

God searches our soul in times of trouble. He needs us to know who we are and who he is. When trouble comes we must seek God for protection; we must hide in his word. We must not allow our spirit to be overtaken by fear but by a song of deliverance while we are yet going through. It is by our coming and going that we learn of God. We must try him for ourselves. It is by experience that faith and trust grows. You must, you must…trust God, have faith in God, know God and know what his word says about him as well as yourself. As I toil, God promises to breathe new life and energy into my spirit. He will renew my spirit while I wait, so that I will not be weary. He will keep my ears tuned to his voice and more important than that…he will keep my tongue in line with his word. It is so important that during times of attack or trial that I speak life and not death. I speak prosperity and not need. I speak health and healing and not sickness. I speak peace to my soul and not confusion. I speak victory in Jesus name and not defeat to the evil one. For my ways and my actions will follow what I say. I must know the enemy will attack from the outside but my healing comes from that which God has placed on the inside. (Help, Holy Spirit) The power of life and death lies in the power of the tongue in a child of God.

Know your purpose in God and speak life to those things that he has promised you. Do not allow the enemy to wear you down, change your mind or turn you around. God has not altered his plan for you one bit; it is you who has altered your plan with God. You have allowed adversity to talk to you and you are listening as it magnifies itself. But hold up! Stop right there! Silence that voice! Magnify God! It is time that the conversation turns to: Oh, what a Mighty God I Serve. Get ye behind me for I am believing what God says about this thing. I know that I can depend on God to deliver me, to protect me, to vindicate me, to bring me through because he is my God. He did it for my brother David many times and he will do the same thing (the exact same thing) for you and me. Hallelujah. Hallelujah. He will do it for me. Oh, yes, he will. I know because I've tried him for myself. As I go through, I walk in the shelter of the Most High. As I go through, I rest in the shadow of the almighty. As I go through, I will trust in the Lord with all my heart and lean not on my own understanding. As I go through,

I will acknowledge the Lord as my shepherd, I will hear his voice. As I go through, I will allow him once again to restore my soul. As I go through, I will call on him and he will hear me; he will answer me. I may be shaken but I will not be consumed. I may be battered but I will not be broken. I may be hurt but I will not be shattered. I may be tempted but I will not fall. I may want to surrender, but I will not, for I hold the victory in God. I am reminded that "This battle is not mine, it is the Lord's. We are Blessed in the Lord.

Gavis Mosley

# BE STRONG IN THE LORD

Joshua 1:9 God says, "Be strong and courageous! Do not tremble or be dismayed, for the Lord your God is with you wherever you go." There is no need to fear when God has already promised us his presence. As we change and things change about us we must seek assurance in the word of God.

Journey with me to the book of Joshua chapters 1-3. We see an important shift taking place. Moses has died and the Lord is calling Joshua to lead his people across the Jordan River into the Promised Land. As a child born into slavery, Joshua knew the power of God. His name alone means "Jehovah is Salvation." Being born into slavery, the first son of Nun, tagged Joshua to be killed during the Passover, yet he was not. He learned early in life that God loved and cared for his people. He knew God as a deliverer as he witnessed the parting and the crossing that took place at the Red Sea. He knew God as one who would fight the battle and conquer the enemy. He knew God as a provider. Joshua was a man of faith. He was mighty in battle. He knew God as his banner. He trusted God to always go before him. He was a man of great courage for he knew that his victory lies with God. Joshua proved himself to be a mighty warrior yet he was a most humble servant of the Lord. He put his faith and trust in God.

God's first command to Joshua was that he prepare himself and the people to cross over the Jordan River. Along with this command, God gives Joshua a promise that he would give him every place he sets his feet. Oh my! He assures Joshua that no one will be able to stand against him for God himself would be with him. God goes on to tell Joshua to be steadfast and unmovable, to not turn to the left or the right; but to continue in his word. God continued to instruct Joshua on how to prepare in such detail that he would not fail. (Joshua was obedient unto the Lord.)

God allowed Joshua to find favor with the people...the Israelites. God had prepared the people as well; for as Joshua began to instruct them, they did not question nor rebel against him. They answered him saying, "Whatever you have commanded us we will do, and wherever you send us we will go." (Now, that's what I call being on one accord, a common purpose for the Lord. Obedience is in action.) When God is in it; there is no limit to that which can be achieved.

Joshua continued in the favor of man as he sent spies to Shittim. They were to look at the land which they had been instructed to take. On the way, they stopped at Rahab's for refuge. The King of Jericho had heard that there were spies in the land and had ordered them captured. But God, he had already intervened on behalf of his people. The spies formed a covenant, an agreement of protection with Rahab. Won't God do it? Here again, we see when God is for you, who can be against you? The spies completed their task unharmed.

We see an entire generation of people dying out before the promise of God is fulfilled. Sometimes it requires the death of the old to occur before the new can spring forth. Often we must be reminded that it is not a matter of age but a matter of faith.

We must know that there were those who were content just living on the edge. They were obedient but satisfied with the edge. This would be the 2 ½ tribes that had been allowed to settle under the leadership of Moses. (Some folks will get just so close, and loose the desire to make it on in. Some folks will never experience their fullness of God due to their spirit of "just enough".) God desires that we have his fullness. This is why it took so long for them to experience the crossing of the Jordan. God desired that all things be new in the Promised Land.

A lesson to be learned here is that we will not come into that which God has for us until we are willing to let go of all those things that serve to hinder us or hold us back. What we need to know and accept is that "letting go" is a process. We must come to obey by our spirit for the flesh (by nature) is not willing to do what is right. The flesh is the child of disobedience. God wants us to allow him to remove the old man and replace it with the new. When he does the work, it will be complete.

The key to receiving the promises of God is obedience. Acts of obedience allowed Moses to part the Red Sea. Those same acts of obedience allowed Joshua to do the same at the Jordon River. (Living proof…if God did it before he will do it again.) And in each case, I should note, the very presence of God was with them. There is no safer or more powerful place to be than in the presence of God. There is no greater place to be than under the Grace of God.

There is no experience like that when you receive the mercy of God.

As you journey towards that which God has promised you; enter his presence with praise, thanksgiving and a spirit of obedience. For when in the presence of God, he is Jehovah, Lord. He is El Shaddai, he has power over all things in our life. He is Jehovah Jireh; he will provide for us so that we will not be in lack for anything. He is Jehovah-Rapha, our healer of body, mind and soul. He is Jehovah-Nissi, our banner that goes before us where ever we may go, that provides us protection and victory. He is Jehovah-Shalom for he gives us peace. He is all we need.

As we are called into obedience, we will experience the victories that God has for us just as he had for those who have gone before us. He is preparing us just as he prepared them, if only we obey. Obedience to God is submission to his word, his will and his way.

God is El-Olam. He is without beginning and ending. He is everlasting. The promises of God were fulfilled in the lives of our forefathers. We experience an even greater promise for we have the ultimate promise living with us. He is alive and ever present. We have a greater presence of God within us. Let's obey, be victorious, and possess all that God has promised us. His word is everlasting to everlasting.

On this journey, be strong and courageous! Do not tremble or be dismayed, for the Lord your God is with you wherever you go. Be blessed in the Lord.

# DON'T LOOK BACK

What can keep me from looking back; nothing, but the blood of Jesus. For, I have been crucified from the world. Without the cross, I am nothing; for it was the cross that gave me deliverance from the world and the things of the world. I have peace with God. In order that I not look back, I must always focus on the cross and all that was done there for me. Because Jesus died for me, I am free and experience liberty.

God desires to show you your future and all he has for you; Satan wants to remind you of your past and all those things that may hinder you. God shows you a portrait so beautifully designed by his word. Satan gives you a snapshot of deceit that will land you in hell's fire. God promises you a life of joy and abundance; Satan promises you that he will kill, steal and destroy all those things that have been designed to build you up.

This I know, I won't go back to the way it used to be, for I have experienced the joy, the power, and the love of Jesus. In Jesus, I am no longer bound. As I understand, by not looking back; I am in the world but no longer of the world. I have been transformed by the renewing of my mind. It is the finished work of Jesus on the cross that keeps me from looking back. Satan can often get one to glimpse back but it is God who keeps us from staring.

There is a lesson to be learned when we are tempted to look back. (What does God say?) First, when I look back, I am not showing my appreciation to God for whom he is and all that he has done. I liken it to a spiritual slap in the face. Journey with me to a story that tells of the fate of one who looked back; it is an insult to God that we would desire to return to a lifestyle of deliberate sin.
If we look back (stare, longing) then it is as if we never left in our heart. My spirit speaks to tell of the experience of one who looked back in Genesis…chapter 19. It is a familiar story but one that has a warning we must heed always…look upon God so that our past will not capture our heart.

Here we see, Lot and his family in the city of Sodom and Gomarrah. The setting of this scene is at the close of day. Two angels entered the city. They were going to stay in the open court for the evening. Lot having seen them arrive offered them shelter in his home for he knew the neighborhood upon which the angels had come. At first the angels did not accept but finally agreed to go the Lot's home for the night. Before day, the sinful men of the city came to the door demanding that Lot turn over the angels to them, that they might have sex with them…my, my, my. They became furious when Lot did not give them over. Lot offered the men his virgin daughters of which they refused. This reveals the hardening of the heart and strong desire to fill the lust of the flesh. As they began to pressure their way forward…the angels pulled Lot inside, made plans to have his family removed from such a sinful place, and then they would destroy the city. As he gathered up his family…his wife, daughters and a few others…the angels had but one command… go and don't look back. Genesis 19:17 says "Escape for thy life, look not behind thee." Lot and his family were leaving a place full of destruction, a place of sin, a place of total disobedience to the word and the works of God. It was a place destined to be destroyed. As he and his family were being led away, they was leaving a very comfortable life of material things, a life that they had become accustomed to, a lifestyle that had taken them away from the path on which God had for them. They were being led out of a place that God deemed no longer worthy to exist.

As they were walking out of the world standard and into a new life with Jesus, Lot's wife was not eager to leave for her heart was not ready. She was taken by the things of the world; so her heart lingered. With the security of her life and family at stake, she yet lingered. She had the promise of a more abundant life before her, yet she lingered. She lingered so in the comfort of a lifestyle of sin, she longed for what was behind her so much that she could not allow her heart to change. Woe unto her. As she was being led out…she looked back…in her heart she longed for the things of the world more that he longed for the love of God. It was at this moment she was turned to a pillar of salt…an ever-present reminder that looking back can keep you from moving forward in the Lord.

Oh, I thank you Lord for the blood that was shed on the cross. For it gives me power, wonder working power to turn away, to die daily to my own desires and live for you. Lord, I thank you as your spirit speaks liberty. I thank you that I am free to worship you. I worship and adore you. Father, today I stand on your promises. I live by your word and I seek your protection from the enemy. As I dwell in your presence, I thank you for being my refuge, my strength, and my redeemer. I thank you that you have restored and continue to restore your spirit upon me. As I worship you in spirit and truth, I need you to know that I love you more than anything. Thank you for your love, your joy and your salvation. Lord, I ask that you move me in the way that you would have me to go. I ask that you help me stay in your word. Any contrite spirit, I ask that you remove it from me. Anything that is not pleasing to you, I ask that you remove it right now. Lord, thank you for seeing the best in me, that you would lead me out of the world and keep me in your care. Lord, thank you for making me sure. Lord, I thank you that you are ordering my steps.

If anyone is in Christ he is a new creature, old things have passed away and all things have become new. Jesus did everything on the cross that was required that we may walk in victory today. We, as children of God, should not look back with hearts that long for the old man or anything that pertains to him. We have all we need today as we can go to our Father and ask with a sincere heart according to his will. He will grant anything that we ask.

When tempted to look back…look up unto the hills from which cometh all your help. Be blessed in the Lord.

# ENDOW ME

I thank you Lord that you found me worth fighting for!

"Endow me, O Lord. In your presence, there is fullness of joy. As I ask you Lord to overtake me, shower down on me your anointing; as I lift you up in praise, I ask the more of you and the less of me. I look to heaven for relief. On this day, Father, you have blessed my spirit anew. You have blessed me with a fresh anointing in your word, you have freshened my walk with thee. You have sharpened, refined, purified, and redefined my inner most for your service. As my thoughts began to wonder, it was your desire that I be touched by your spirit. It was your desire that I be touched, arrested and called back into your fold. I know that I am being called and you have prepared me for a deeper assignment in you. You are calling me to move out of my comfort zone and into yours. You have called me out of tradition and into practice. Oh Lord, my strength, my redeemer."

As I journey, I am taken to a promise…" If you love Me, you will keep My commandments. And I will ask the Father, and he will give you another Counselor to be with you forever – the Spirit of Truth. He will live with you and in you. He will teach you all

things and will remind you of everything I have said to you."
Oh, what a promise! But, what does it really mean to you?

Jesus promised us that God would send us a comforter who would take his place. Jesus's ministry here on earth was but for a short time; but the deliverance of the Holy Spirit would have an everlasting effect in the life of the believer. It means that we would have Christ living inside of us, to lead us, guide us, to continue to teach us the will of God the Father. It would be through our obedience to the Holy Spirit and by our knowledge of the word of God that we would come to know him.

I see Jesus as he is teaching and praying with his disciples. He announces to them that the word must be fulfilled. He tells them that he will be leaving them soon. Of course, they are deeply distressed at the news of their being left alone. Jesus in his love and care for them reveals a deeper truth…that of the Holy Spirit. He lets them know that they will not be alone but that they will receive his essence in the form of the Holy Spirit to live eternally within.

What does this mean, again I ask, to you and me? Well…it means hope for a brighter day; it means peace in the valley. It means comfort in your times of trouble. It means a renewed mind during a corrupt world. It means we now can live an acceptable life before the Lord God. It means one day, we will meet him face-to-face never to know sorrow again. It means no more tears. No more pain. Every day will be dedicated to praising his holy name. Jesus's promise was made perfect (complete) on the Day of Pentecost. The Holy Spirit came and embodied itself in the disciples and taught them the more of Jesus the Christ. Thus, he does the same for you and me today.

In a culture filled with moral and spiritual regression, we are called to look to the scriptures for encouragement. We must know what the word of God says about righteous living. We must know that it is possible to do the next right thing. However, we must know that we cannot do this in and of ourselves, we must depend on and trust in the Lord.

The very nature of man is captured in Romans Chapter 7. Paul speaks frankly to the believer "I do not understand what I do. For what I want to do I do not do, but what I hate I do." "I know that nothing good lives in me, that is, in my sinful nature. For I have the desire to do what is good, but I cannot carry it out." But there is a change that takes place with the endowing of the Holy Spirit. All things are made possible through Jesus Christ. Paul gives us these words of encouragement as well: Everyone is tempted of the evil one, so you are not alone in the struggle. Everyone does not fall into temptation. We can resist any temptation not by our might but by the word of God and the spirit that dwells within us.

Man, in and of himself has no true knowledge of the truth, of right and wrong. Man left to himself will literally self-destruct. The flesh hungers for the things of the world, of the evil one. Our eyes lust after material gain naturally; thus, we hunger for it. We will do anything and everything to achieve them in the flesh. Our moral character in the flesh would be no more than animalistic. We would hunt each other down without remorse; that is what the flesh would do! But God, he has given us a chance at new life in the spirit. That's why Jesus was manifested in the flesh, came to earth and journeyed with man so that we would have an opportunity to live eternally with him.

It is the Holy Spirit that allows us to recognize that person, place or thing that leads us into temptation. When that thing comes upon us, we are called to flee (run and run fast), for we do not want to be overtaken. The mature in the Lord can look that demon in the face and in the strength of the Lord send that demon back into the pits of hell. Note, I said the mature in the Lord! It begins with a desire to do right, to be righteous. We must know that doing the wrong thing only leads us to defeat. When we get weak, we have only to pray to God for his help. He is faithful and true to being there for us. Obeying God, doing his will is not impossible; it has been made possible by the Holy Spirit.

The Holy Spirit gives us the power and authority to walk as Christ walked. We have the power to overcome the lures of this world; so that which the flesh desires will not overtake us. It will be the Holy Spirit that keeps us and not our flesh. He will be that one who controls us when we are tempted to walk contrary to the word of God. He causes us to be grateful for just another day of new grace and mercy. He keeps us from losing our mind when the world turns its back on us and we feel all alone. He will keep us from being the biggest liars, cheaters, and back biters in town. He can help change your life…from being a dishonest person to be a faithful husband or wife…from being mentally unstable to be an advocate for the mentally challenged and oppressed…from being an unfair tax collector to be a financial advisor. The Holy Spirit changes our way of thinking. He will ease the pain of heartbreak. He will comfort us more than a mother's touch. He will be our guiding force by day and by night, in times of joy and in times of sorrow. He will continuously teach us the difference in right and wrong as well as the benefits of grace and mercy. He will help us to understand the ways of the one whom we serve. He will be our interpreter. He will promote us in wisdom. He will be our strength in times of weakness. He will stand up as our strong tower. He will give us the boldness to stand before the enemy and proclaim Jesus as Lord of our lives. He is our intercessor. He will keep us safe and secure as we journey to and fro throughout this world. He will hold us until Jesus returns.

Lord, endow me with thy spirit. Amen.

Gavis Mosley

# ENJOY THE JOURNEY

I am called to encourage you. Despite everything that you've been through, you are still able to say, "Thank You".

Know that you serve a living God that know all things about you. He knows your name. All that we encounter has been designed for us by him, for our good; for he made us for his purpose. God has already established you. God wants you to know that you are the redeemed.

Jeremiah 1:5 says "before I formed you in the womb I knew you (therefore nothing in our life has been a surprise to him), before you were born I set you apart; (God set us apart for his service knowing the journey that we would travel before we would accept him…that's awesome); I appointed you as a prophet to the nations." God knew before you were born what you would have the capacity to become because he had already defined and refined you. Our potential lies in God not in us and what we perceive it to be. That's why it's so important that we get in tune and stay in tuned to the word of God. God knows what's within each of us. Psalms 139:13 says "For you, created my inmost being, you knit me together in my mother's womb."

As we journey we are often caught up in ourselves. We begin to limit our abilities according to our capacity to handle the situations of life. In doing so, we are limiting the vision that God has for us. God is the author and creator of our faith; he determines what we can bear, what we can and cannot do. On this journey from the sunshine to the rain, from times of celebration to times of pain, we are called to worship the Lord. Key to the journey is the word and promises of God.

Joshua 1:9 lets me know that I don't have to be afraid. I can step out on the word of God will be with me. "Have I not commanded you? Be strong and courageous. Do not be afraid, do not be discouraged, for the Lord your God will be with you wherever you go." As God speaks and directs you, he wants you to move in the assurance of his word, of his promises. Let's back up to verse 8 where it reads, "This book of the law shall not depart from your mouth, but you shall meditate on it day and night, so that you may be careful to do according to all that is written in it, for then you will make your way prosperous, and then you will have success." God has a plan for reach of us and it is spelled out in his word.

Journey with me as I mediate on the word and the promises of God. He doesn't want us to give up on our dreams, to doubt the future that he has promised us. If God is for us nothing can ever stop us. He desires that we speak to our mountains and not allow our mountains to speak to us.

The book of Joshua begins with the home going of Moses. The people have known and respected Moses as a faithful leader who was led by God. His torch is now passed onto Joshua. Fulfillment of the promises of God lay with and in Joshua's faith and belief in the word and promises of God. It lay in his courage and in his trust.

Joshua has shown himself to be a courageous warrior as well as a faithful servant. Joshua has been commissioned to lead God's people into the promise land. It's been a long time coming. They have wondered around in the wilderness for 40 years. There's a word here that speaks never give up, never let go, don't allow the passing of time to get you down. For God, is incapable of letting you down. Often times God uses our wilderness experiences to build us, strengthen us, and prepare us for his purpose. Time is often used to cleanse and separate. This is the case with Joshua. (You and I). We must be careful of those that we carry with us into our promise from God. We must leave behind those who weigh us down with disbelief and doubt and carry with those who stand with us on the word of God.

Joshua has seen the hand of God. Now, he is being called to walk by faith. Down through the years, Joshua has learned that God is all powerful. He has witnessed the goodness of God. He was a witness to the plagues in Egypt that caused Pharaoh to release the people. He was a witness to the crossing at the Red Sea and the destruction of the enemy. He was a witness to God's provision as they wandered in the wilderness. He never waived, he stood and waited in anticipation of the glory of God being fulfilled.

Another thing, Joshua knew that God was with him. For in his word he declared to Joshua " As I was with Moses, so I will be with you, I will never leave you nor forsake you…Do not be terrified;

do not be discouraged, for the Lord your God will be with you wherever you go." When God speaks a move in your spirit then we should not doubt but should rise and proceed forward in boldness and assurance.

It was Joshua who led the people of God into the Promise Land. The word and promise of God was made complete by a mighty and faithful servant. God speaks the same to you and me today. He wants us to be mighty and faithful to him in all that we do. We are called to consider every mountain that God has brought us to. We are called to consider every valley that he has walked us through. We are called to celebrate every victory that life has given us. We are called to worship and praise him in spirit and truth. As we consider the word of God, we are called to take a careful and detail look at the man in the mirror and just consider what does his works mean to you.

Our relationship with God is one that is unique to us. We can expect and anticipate God to do all that he says he will do and more. God desires that we possess that Promise Land that he has for us. As for me until that day comes…I'm going to enjoy my journey for this I know…that no weapon formed against me will prosper, greater is he who is in me than he who is in the world. I know that come what may, if God allows it to come to me, he has already prepared me to stand. I know that I serve a faithful, living God who is incapable of failing me. I know that I walk by faith and not by sight so the things I see in the physical will not hinder the power of my spirit. I know that as I go to and fro he goes before me in all things. I know that in my most troubled time he will never leave me nor forsake me. I know that he is near me. I know him as my provider. I know him as protector. When I hurt, I know him as comforter. When I allow my thoughts to haunt me, I know him as my mind regulator, my redeemer. He is my peace maker. He allows me to rebuke the accuser with my praise. I know that in him I'm more than a conqueror. I know that he equips those that he calls. I know that just as he kept his promises to Joshua; he'll do the same for me. I know that in him my name is Victory. As I turn the more to him…I love him and he loves me. As I anchor in him…I will…Enjoy the journey. Amen!

Gavis Mosley

# FORGIVE ME

As I shed the old and put on the new, I am being transformed into the new life. Change brings with it a wealth of emotions. My perspective is not determined by what I see with my physical eyes but by that which I cannot see. I believe on that which is yet to be. I believe by faith in Jesus. I seek my hidden treasure. The treasure that God and God alone has stored for me. For it is my time.

On this journey, as I think of change and being transformed, my thoughts lead me to forgiveness. I have had to learn to forgive. (A task that is easier said than done.) "I forgive you" …3 words so often spoken but so hard to do. To forgive someone means to put aside. To forgive someone is to forget their trespass against you. To forgive means that the hurt, the pain, the guilt is no longer in the heart. It means that I no longer harbor a hard feeling against that person. It means that I can meet you with a genuine smile on my heart. I know what I said. I need a smile on my heart not on my face. I know oh so well that that facial smile can and will be turned on and off like a switch, up or down, on or off. I can be so fake. But when my heart has been changed, healed, restored…there's no faking. For the issues of life lie in the heart. I must forgive (have a change of heart) in order that I be forgiven.

My journey leads me to the cross. On a hill far away, my Savior was crucified and died for me. One who came and stood blameless before man, gave up his life. One who knew no sin; gave up his life in order that I may win. My Savior is Jesus Christ. One who was tested and tried; yet he came forth white as snow. For you see, my Savior was designed to turn his head and offer the other cheek. My Savior is one who loved me while I was still a servant of the enemy. I was lost but he left that which he knew to find me and bring me unto him. He desired to forgive me and make me whole.

I have once again been given another chance. Another. Another. And yet another. I am so grateful that when Peter asked Jesus how many times was he to forgive; seven times? Jesus answered, "No, seventy-seven times." We should forgive according to the love, grace and mercy that by which we have been forgiven. Have you even given thought to the many times that you have had to ask for forgiveness?

Journey with me to the book of Matthew, Chapter 18. It speaks of a king who desired to settle his debt with his servants. As he began to settle his accounts, he came to a servant who owed him ten thousand talents. The king ordered that the servant and his family be sold to repay the debt. The servant fell to his knees and asked for patience (forgiveness). The king had mercy and cancelled the debt and let him go. This same servant went out and encountered a servant who owed him. The fellow servant pleaded with him for patience but he was not forgiven. The forgiven servant was not forgiving. He ordered that the indebted servant be put in jail. As others looked on, they became distressed and reported what had happened to the king. The king was outraged. He called in the servant he had forgiven and had him tortured. Woe, unto you who are forgiven but do not have the heart to forgive. Woe unto you.

Now journey with me back to the cross. How can we not forgive our fellow man when we look upon the cross? What cause do we have to hold a grievance against one another? Think about it. Mediate on it. Pray to God for a change of heart. Know that when we forgive, we will be forgiven even more. Rejoice in knowing that God lives so that we may live.

For as he hung his head and gave up his life…a final request was breathed…'Father, forgive them, for they know not what they do' What a request for you. What a request for me. Think. Pray. Mediate. You are forgiven. Be forgiving. Be blessed in the Lord.

# GOD'S HAND

I'm looking for a miracle, a breakthrough, a breaking and falling away of chains, a shift, a move of the atmosphere. I'm believing for more of Jesus. I'm holding on to the stone, the foundation, and the rock of my salvation. I'm waiting, oh but while I wait…

I've come to believe that there's nobody like Jesus, Jesus, the very Son of God desires that we come into his presence and receive of him. It is in his presence that we receive the spirit of comfort, assurance, deliverance and strength. For the Lord our God is mighty in battle, he hung the sun, the moon and the stars. It is he who said let there be as it was so. My desire to be closer has gotten the attention of the enemy. I pray now that I am able to see the guiding hand of God as I journey to that secret place to still away with him…

I am reminded of the word found in Jeremiah where it says "For I know the plans I have for you, "declares the Lord," plans to prosper you and not to harm you, plans to give you hope and a future". Even the more, I hear you speak to the prophet…"Go down to the potter's house and there I will give you my message."

(God desires that we see him and his hand at work clearly in our lives). So I went down to the potter's house. (Obedience to the word of God is the key to answered prayers). And I saw him working at the wheel, but the pot he was shaping from the clay was marred in his hands; so the potter formed it into another pot, shaping it as seemed best to him."

Here we are in the hands of God with all our limitations and imperfections. Here we are before the Lord asking him to take us and make us all over again. Here we are once again asking God to fix us and to make us whole, yet we are doing as we do complaining and wanting things to go our way through it all. Lord help us to give you our broken pieces, our thoughts of insecurity, our tears and heartache. Sift us like flour, sanctify us Lord. Squeeze us Jesus so the oil that you have placed in us will flow freely. As we spin Father, you know our hurt, our discomfort, our heart, soul and mind. As we die to our flesh, we will rejoice in the spirit. Help us to endure as you bless us with patience, trust, long-suffering, kindness, meekness, love, dependence and assurance. Shape us Lord for only you know best.

We are all a work under construction. God, the potter, is at work in our lives revealing to us just who he is and his control over all things. God sees our imperfections and shortcomings, our jealousies and envy. He sees our fear and our anger. He looks ever so closely on our prejudice and judgement. Then, he allows us to be made over again, in his hands. In the process, he plucks out bitterness and puts in a touch of honey from the honeycomb. He refines our hate and envy into meekness and gentleness. As we rebel, he pulls us in, to hold us just a little closer, and then speeds up the wheel. Here he is giving us definition and purpose. As the wheel begins to slow down, he gives us an opportunity to gather our senses and a portion of understanding so that we will be able to absorb all that we have gone through in his hand. It is then we are prepared to get down off the wheel and follow our God in spirit and in truth for our steps have now been ordered.

They have been ordered by the one and only living God. One who sits high and looks low. One whom no one can separate you from his love. There's no place that you can go and he's not already there. He's our ever-present help. He's always on time, he's never been late. He goes before us and has prepared a place for us. He loves us and keeps us. He gives us comfort and assurance. All that we will ever be and all that we will ever need is just a touch away…in God's hand.

Gavis Mosley

# GOD WILL PROVIDE

Psalms 145:9 reads…The Lord is God to all; he has compassion on all he has made.

I will trust in you Lord. I will always be careful to honor and obey your ways. I will call on you, your holy name in times of distress as well as in times of celebration. I have come to know you as faithful, as all that I need. One of my most frightening thoughts is of…where would I be in life without you.

Lord, I thank you, as you lift me up above the troubles of my past, above the anxiety of my today and above the uncertainty of my tomorrow. You lift me so that I may see the assurance that lies in you. It's you whom I seek. You, who is in control of "the then", "the now" and "the forever".

I had yet another awesome opportunity to sit and share with my grandmother today. The word of God through David spoke to my heart as she told of times during her 95 years here on earth. They come from Psalms 37:25, "I was young and now I am old, yet I have never seen the righteous forsaken or their children begging bread."

I began to look past the physical as God revealed the spirit of those words to my inner being. She spoke of times when she and her friends and family walked miles to get where they were going. It would take them hours to get from place to place. They walked often in the heat of the day as well as in the darkness of the night. They walked not on a paved road but through woods. Real trees and forest woods. She spoke of pieces of fat meat to eat, corn meal bread and fresh milk with butter in it (straight from the cow…churning) being the meal of the day. And, they were glad to get it. She spoke of doing chores for a dime then going to the store and what she could buy with such a small amount of money to care for not just herself but her family. (Look at God). He has seen her from a day of lack to a day of more than enough.

Her words alone are a testimony of the goodness and the faithfulness of God. She spoke of how her mother took a little of nothing and made it into just enough. It goes without saying that God worked through her mother and made a way. As she spoke of how her father put her on a train and how far they walked to get there, and then of how far he would have to walk back alone at night. My eyes filled with tears as I looked upon her face. She smiled, knowing how deeply he loved her and cared for her to do such a thing.

What more do we have with our heavenly father? What more does he care and provide? What more?

God cares for us and he loves us. We should put all our hope, faith and trust in him. My grandmother now lives a comfortable life. It is truly by the grace, mercy and faithfulness of God. He's the same God of her corn meal bread and fat meat days. I'm so grateful that she has shared him with me. As she sits threading straws making a basket, she too is weaving pieces of straw within me so that I may carry and hold on to…straw pieces of hope, love, faithfulness and dependence in the Lord. In her sharing, I see the provision and protection of God. I see his patience and long suffering. But most of all, I see his love and his care.

I'm taken to the word of God in 1 Kings Chapter 17. There it speaks of Elijah and the widow at Zarepath. God sent Elijah there for food and refuge. When he gets there, he encounters a widow. She is collecting sticks for a fire to cook her last meal for herself and her son. She has run out of supplies and there is no hope for her to receive more. She's at her end and is preparing to give up and die. She's lost all hope for a better day. Now, here comes this man asking her for her last. Really? But, there is a word from the Lord…Elijah tells her to not be afraid but to do as he asks for God has promised him that her jars will not be empty. Now, this widow has a choice to make…to prepare the meal for Elijah and take a chance on dying hungry or trust in the word from the Lord. As we know, her jars were never empty again. She could carry on for God did provide.

My grandmother and this widow stand because of the goodness, the protection, the provision, the faithfulness and the love given by the Lord.

God has a word for each of us. We have only to trust and obey for he is faithful.

Come what may, he has, he is and he shall provide. Amen.

Gavis Mosley

# KEEPING OUR EYES ON THE LORD

I've come to praise the Lord my God, Jesus my redeemer and the Holy Spirit my interpreter. I give God all the glory for he is worthy to be praised. We should always praise the Lord. It is God who wakes us daily. It is God who comes to give us strength and courage in the midnight hour. It is God who is able to heal our bodies and comfort our spirit. It is God who speaks to us when no other word can be heard. It is the word and promises of God that can speak to the troubled heart. It is God.

As I worship, I am encouraged for I know that God is working things out. I can worship because my faith lies in the word of God. God says that he will never leave me nor forget about me. He says that I should be anxious for nothing but in all things seek him. He tells me to pray without ceasing so that my mind, body and soul would be lifted up. I am encouraged for he is the keeper of my soul.

For such a time as this, it's good to know that I have a friend in Jesus. Lord, I'm so grateful to be able to praise you for there is a distraction in my life right now that is trying to steal my praise. In the midst of it all, I'm so grateful that things are as well as they are. I'm grateful because the foundation of my faith is Jesus Christ.

"Lord I pray that you make me strong as I go through this season. Make me strong in you. Help me to speak your word with boldness and assurance, as I stand and decree by faith. Lord, I pray strength and restoration as a testimony of your goodness to the faithful. I pray that you breathe life anew on my brothers in Jesus name. Send down your ministering angels. I come as one who lives in the hope that you have so generously given me. My hope lies in you. I know there's nothing too hard for you. I pray, I petition your throne for restoration. I declare and decree by the same power that you called "out "to Lazarus you will do the same in this season for those who are waiting on you. I petition you Lord, the God of Daniel in the lion den…the God of the three Hebrew boys who you saved from the fiery furnace…the God of the healed leper who returned to give thanks…the God of the woman at the well whose sins were forgiven…the God of Paul one who boldly proclaimed your name and spoke mighty of your goodness…the God of the woman with the issue of blood who was healed by just touching the hem of your garment…Oh Lord you are able to speak life, strength and restoration. And as I pray, Lord help me to not be distracted.

"Live on" echoes in my spirit. We are called to praise and worship God, for it is there, that we will receive our blessing, our breakthrough, our deliverance and our answers to prayers. As I have shared the events of this season, repeatedly I've spoken of the goodness of God and how he continues to show up in such a mighty way. Yet, there have been plenty of periods of distractions.

Come what may I'm still called to stay focus on the true and living God. I'm called to praise and worship the Lord.

On this journey, we will have distractions. A distraction is something that makes it difficult to think or pay attention to that which you know you should be paying attention to. It is something that amuses or entertains you to keep your mind off of what's important. In the life of the believer distractions come in many forms, mainly, they come to make us doubt the promises of God. Let's not be distracted but let us all praise and worship the Lord. In your praise and worship release your fears, doubts and unbelief and God will meet you just where you are. He will strengthen, encourage and revive you for the task at hand. Free yourself from those things that come to hinder you from focusing on the word, the power, the majesty and the authority of God. Lord help us to trust you the more. Help us to listen for your voice as we seek your wisdom in our season of test, trial and distraction. (They do travel together you know.)

Lord, thank you for allowing me to see your compassion and love as I feel pain. I see you revealing your wisdom in a time when confusion is all around. I see you being a loving Father. I see this same love, compassion and guidance in your word. For as we journey and become distracted by the cares of this world and all that comes with it...you are still near and continue to catch us and bring us lovingly back to you.

I'm taken to the book of Matthew, Chapter 14, verses 13-36. It speaks to the distraction of man and the steadfastness, the focus of Jesus. Within this passage you see Jesus retreating to a remote area to pray. He is followed there by many people. It was here that he fed 5000 men, not including the women and children. The disciples wanted to send the people away for they were distracted by the limitation of humanity. However Jesus was focused on the majesty of divinity. Immediately after he fed the people he sent the disciples away in a boat. He sent the people away and went on a mountainside to pray. During the night, a storm arose and the wind began to toss the boat. As Jesus went out to be with them, they were afraid for they were in the midst of a storm and could not recognize Jesus coming out to them. They thought he was a ghost. (This is often what happens to us.)

We get so distracted with the thing that is coming against us; that we forget to call on the Lord of all. As he comes to us in his own way often we fail to see him working in the process, especially if it doesn't happen according to our thoughts or ideas). Jesus immediately spoke peace to them and said "Take courage! It is I. Don't be afraid." Then Peter said, "If it's you Lord, tell me to come to you on the water." At this point, Peter is totally focus on Jesus. He knows that Jesus is near. "Come." Jesus said. The word of God tells me that Peter got out of the boat and walked on the water towards Jesus. But...he got distracted. The same things happens to you and me. On this journey, unless we are careful, our focus can be shifted. When he saw the wind, felt the water underneath his feet and began to look at his humanity, his ability...he was afraid and began to sink. Peter cried out to Jesus and immediately Jesus reached out his hand and caught him. It is in those moments of distraction, when we take our eyes off Jesus our spirits cry out in fear. "You of little faith," Jesus said, "Why did you doubt?" We must know that we can do all things, and endure all things, even distractions, through Christ who strengthens us.

We are called to keep our eyes on God. There's nothing too hard for our God and there's nothing he won't do for us. We must put all of our faith, trust and hope in God, come what may. Distractions will cause us to question the authority of Jesus. They will cause us to minimize the power of our Savior. They will cause us to question his love and care for us. They will cause us to doubt his integrity and character. It's even more important to recognize where you are and get back on track with the one and living God. He's the only one who can give you the peace, comfort, security, love and care that you are seeking. He is God.

As I pray, "Lord, as I stand I know it is within your power to speak "Rise Brother", "Rise Brother" and walk, and it would be so. I know this because you are the one and true living God. My brothers, I pray that you know his eyes are on the sparrow and know that he's watching over you. He's a good God and he's faithful. He's the same yesterday, today, and tomorrow. To you my loves, I say hold on and wait on the Lord, for he is near. Wait I say, wait on the Lord. My brothers don't' be distracted by what you're going through for God has many promises for you…But they who wait for the Lord shall renew their strength; they shall mount up on wings like eagles; they shall run and not be weary; they shall walk and not faint…In your heart speak "I believe that I shall look upon the goodness of the Lord in the land of the living! Wait for the Lord! Be strong and let your heart take courage; Wait for the Lord!"…Touch and agree "Our soul waits for the Lord; He is our help and our shield. For our heart is glad in him, because we trust in his holy name. Let your steadfast love, O Lord, be upon us, even as we hope in you. Amen"

Today, I won't be distracted. I'm going to keep looking to the Lord.

# MORE THAN ENOUGH

Father God, I thank you for being my joy, my shelter, my strength, my comforter, my protection. My spirit sings, "Just look at the blessing, what the Lord has done for me."

When others said that it was over for me, God said he wasn't finished with me. When others said that I was just wasting my life away, God said he was preparing a mighty woman of God with a testimony. As the enemy comes against me, God says that I am more than a conqueror.

I am taken to John 6:12. There Jesus said to his disciples "Gather the pieces that are leftover. Let nothing be wasted."

These words were spoken by Jesus after he fed the crowd of 5000. The word of God tells me in John 6:13, he fed the gathering from a lunch of two small fish and five loaves of bread. Jesus was concerned for the people who had followed him into an open place. He knew they needed physical food to survive their travel; as well, he knew they needed the spiritual food of the word to nourish their souls. Yet, what appeared as not enough in the eyes of man was placed in the care of Jesus. The word says he "blessed" the food, and then distributed it to the people. When Jesus blesses,

he makes a little, more than enough. Each person was filled.
He then instructed his disciples to gather up the leftovers, so that nothing would be wasted. They collected 12 baskets of pieces. Leftovers. Just as Jesus blessed the food, he is blessing us right now. When we begin to think that we have nothing left to offer, we are broken and can't go any further, then is the time when we should turn our leftovers, over to Jesus.

Jesus will pick us up, gather together all the pieces of our lives, and use us for his purpose. He will not allow one of our pieces to be lost. Oftentimes we have plans for our lives; but God has a vision for us that is greater than we can even imagine. We are often distracted by our own desires. Along the way, as Satan would have it, things don't quite go as planned. We end up compromising our values as well as our faith and walk with God to accomplish our goals. In other words, we take it upon ourselves to bless ourselves. We often end up broken in heart and spirit.

"Did it really take all of that?" is a frequent question I ask myself? I say 'yes'. I had to be broken, in order that, I could receive new life in Jesus Christ. I am blessed to have walked through shame and guilt into confidence and respect. I am blessed to have the sound mind to seek my refuge in the word of God instead of in that "thing" that I had grown to depend on as my flesh rose up in me. I am blessed to have survived the trials and tribulations of my circumstance, for now, I am able to give the same comfort to my sisters and brothers as that which was given to me. I know it was God who held the death angels until I could reach my crossroad of circumstance.

God once again met me there and showed me that although I

had changed the path, he was still the destination. Holy Spirit fall fresh on me. I came to him weary, worn, and broken down! Yet, he accepted me, just as I was. And then, he blessed me to not look like what I have been through. The Lord has had mercy on me and I am so grateful. He has restored me unto myself and to him.

He takes me daily into his arms and when I need it most, I can feel him hold me ever so close. As I rest in him, I must trust him today; as he leads me on my journey. I must know that my path was the one assigned for me. For without it, I would not be the person that I am today. The glory of it all is that God was not surprised by what was left of me. He knew when I would come to him and just what I would come with. God knew just what to do with that which was left of me (my pieces, my leftovers).

I am no longer scattered; God has gathered me up and brought me unto him so that I would not be wasted. I no longer must wonder or question my path for in God I have found my destiny. Leftovers…God is blessing my little and making it more than enough.

Come to Jesus today. Allow him to gather you, so that you may be whole again. We are already blessed in the Lord.

# YOU KEPT ME

Lord, I thank you for your "keeping me." I thank you. If anyone else out there has even been kept, I need you to rejoice with me. Praise God with me because we are not headed to hell anymore but we are truly headed to be with our Lord. We are going up yonder to be with our Savior, our giver of life, our comforter, our protector, our redeemer. I can see clearly that which at one time I could vaguely dream of. I now live a life that Satan had convinced me would be impossible. I walk a path that is now straight and narrow, for the wide path had deep ditches that were hard to climb out of. I now look to God for validation and strength for man is too hard to please and he causes me to be weak. Rejoice with me if you have even been "kept" by the Lord.

Lord, I thank you for keeping me from dangers seen and unseen. I thank you for you kept my mind protected as I wondered; for it could have easily been taken by the evil one. Lord, I thank you for I never truly believed the report that man had on my life. I knew you loved me; for you allowed me to stay long enough for me to love and appreciate you. You allowed me to be where I could know for myself what it truly meant to have someone who loves me "unconditionally." I thank you for all my life experiences, all of them, because as we journeyed; it was you, who brought me through. You kept me.

As I journey, I do so in the knowledge of my sisters and brothers in Christ, who have gone before me, in the courage of those I currently walk with and in the hope of those whom I will encounter. For you see, I serve an everlasting to everlasting God. The word of God is never-ending. David, Ruth, Joshua, Ester, Daniel, Rahab…past, present, future…were not and are not defined by time but by the word of God. Ever present help in the time of need. I have learned of them by my study of the word of God. I learned of the many battles of faith and deliverance they all had to fight. I learned of the challenges that brought them to their knees. I learned of the obstacles that brought them to a point of "break". I also learned that at the point of "break" they each had an all-important decision to make.

It was a very personal choice that only they could make for themselves. Each one experienced the terror that night brings. Each one at one time or another feared for their very life. Yet, each one ultimately decided to follow the giver of life. They chose to follow God! They chose to bless the Lord in spite of the trouble that lay before them. They decided to trust what God had revealed to them about their situation. It was truly a decision of faith, of trust and of obedience. God kept them. And, he will keep you.

I challenge you to read and study the word of God. You will find there the answers to all the issues of life. You will find that he is the same God: yesterday, today and tomorrow. (Thank you, Jesus). It gives hope to the hopeless. It gives life to those things that in our own strength we have given up for dead. It will give comfort where there is confusion. It gives protection when you are surrounded by danger on all sides. It will give peace in the midst of the storm. It specializes in rest to the weary. I challenge you to try God. Allow him to keep you.

Psalms 91...empowers me...I will say of the Lord, "He is my refuge and my fortress, my God, in whom I trust." I will see many fall all around me; but if I trust in him, I will be left standing to see the victory. Psalms 23...he is my provider..."The Lord is my shepherd, I shall not be in want."

Jeremiah 29...I no longer have to wonder about my future..."For I know the plans I have for you, declares the Lord, "plans to prosper you and not to harm you, plans to give you hope and a future." Galatians 22...I no longer have to wonder what to wear each day..."But the fruit of the Spirit is love, joy, peace, patience, kindness, goodness, faithfulness, gentleness and self-control." Finally, I am secured...John 3:16..." For God so loved the world that he gave his one and only Son that whoever believes in him shall not perish but have eternal life." He keeps you...in his word.

We must stand on the word of God or we will find ourselves falling for everything and anything. Trust God. Trust God. Trust God. As a child of God, we may feel the fear but our strength is developed when we face the fear head on, walk through the fear and when we come out: our faith and trust in God will be increased. Strength, true strength, comes by our continued and increased faith and trust in God. The spirit of God lives in us; we are prompted to always trust him. We can't always change the way we feel but we can keep that feeling from overtaking us. We can do all things through Christ who strengthens us. In other words, I can feel totally wrong yet (in the Lord) still do the right thing. I may want to say something to someone; however, if it does not profit that person in the Lord, then I must do the right thing and keep my mouth closed. I must wait on the Lord. If I make the right choices as I go through; then there is no devil in hell that can come against me and win.

I say to you, I could not change and you will not change by merely wishing things were different. Change comes by pressing, pressing and more pressing. We must press toward the giver of our faith. Press past the desires of the flesh toward the harvest that has been stored up for you. Experience the goodness of God. Allow him to keep you. Today is a day that the Lord has made; let us rejoice and be glad in it. Let everything that has breath PRAISE THE LORD. Be blessed in the Lord.

# OPEN MY EYES

Lord, open my eyes so that I may see my angels instead of my enemy. Show me your ways, O Lord, teach me your path; guide me in your truth and teach me, for you are God my Savior, and my hope is in you all day long. I lift up my eyes to the hills from which comes my help; for all my help comes from the Lord, the maker of heaven and earth. The earth is the Lord's and everything in it. Blessed are all who take refuge in him. Lord, open my eyes so that I may see.

As believers don't confuse the size of your faith with the bases of your faith, each one's measure of faith is rooted in the Lord. It takes just a mustard seed of faith to move mountains. It is in him that little faith will grow into great faith. It is God's amazing grace that allows us to see him in all things. Journey with me to 2 Kings 6: 8-23. Here we find men of God surrounded by the enemy. (My heart rejoices, for his eyes are on the sparrow, I know he watches over me. Amen.) Here we see the Arameans at war with Israel. As the King of Aram is planning attacks on Israel, God is revealing these plans to Elisha, who is warning the King of Israel. The King of Aram becomes angry and confused to the point where he believes he has a spy in his camp. He questions his officers as to who could be betraying him. One of his officers reveals that there is a man of God who is warning the Israelites of each plan. So the king changes his point of attack away from the Israelites to a personal attack on the man of God. (Who knows that this is not a good thing to do…to touch...to attack...to go against the anointed…the appointed of God?) The King seeks out to capture Elisha. The army moves to Dothan by night and surrounds the place where Elisha is residing.

Know that God is a protector of his people. The servant of Elisha rises early this particular morning and goes outside business as usual; but to his surprise the camp is surrounded by the enemy. (Have you ever gotten up to start your day, and all hell breaks out and you wonder just what is really going on?) The servant of Elisha becomes afraid because he was not prepared or had not expected to be confronted with this attack from the enemy. He becomes focused entirely on what he sees and that is that he is surrounded by a massive army and there seems to be no way out. It appears as though he and his master are about to be overtaken.

As the enemy approaches, he cries out in dread to Elisha, "Oh Lord, what must we do?" Elisha seeks to give him words of comfort and confident. He first tells him to not be afraid. He goes on to say that "those who are with us are more than who are with them." Elisha then prayed to God that he would open the eyes of his servant. He desired that his servant see beyond the problem and know that God was the problem solver. He desired that his servant remember the word of God that says that there is none greater than him. God answered Elisha's prayer, for when the servant looked again, not only did he see the army advancing towards them, but he also saw a band of horses and chariots of fire total surrounding the army of Aram. God had opened his eyes that he may see his angels' protection about him versus the attack of the enemy against him.

As we journey, we must know that we will always be objects of attack by the enemy. It is the job of the enemy to attack believers and he is good at it. Along with this, we must more importantly know that he who is for us is more than he who is against us. We must know that the battle is not ours but it belongs to the Lord who is victorious. On this journey, we must spend time in prayer and meditation, studying the word of God and receiving revelation of the word from God. When the enemy does come against us, we are empowered with the word and fortified by the Holy Spirit which dwells within us. In times such as these, we must pray that God would open our eyes that we may truly see him and his mighty working power. The servant represents us as believers who are not prepared for the spiritual warfare that may come against us. He stepped out business as usual, as we often do, totally unprepared for the attack which awaited him. However, his master Elisha was able to remain calm, comforted and confident for he was anchored in the truths of God. He was aware of the army but he was more focused on what God had to say about this situation; therefore he was able to see the horses and chariots of fire that surrounded the army. His eyes were open to God.

The enemy is defeated by the word of God. Psalm 27: 1-3 says "The Lord is the light and my salvation; whom shall I fear? The Lord is the defense of my life; whom shall I dread? When evildoers come upon me to devour my flesh (being against my emotions, my finances, my health, my faith, my walk with God, my peace, my comfort or my security), My adversaries and my enemies, (be it physical or spiritual) they stumbled and fell. (Notice this is showing past victories in the Lord which produced a greater faith for present challenge. Now look at how I am to respond today. ) Though a host encamp against me, my heart will not fear; though war rise against me, in spite of this, I shall be confident."

Do we hear the doctor's report of illness, sickness and disease, or do we believe the report that by his stripes we are healed? Do we hear the report of the judge that hands down an unfair sentence; or do we petition the throne of grace again and again as the widow who went before the king until he showed her favor? Do we settle for less than God has for us or do we go as Joshua did and possess our promised land of overflow? Do we give in to the threats and darts of the enemy or do we stand as David did and slay our giants? Do we walk around hopeless and in despair, feeling incomplete, wondering if there is anyone who cares, or do we step out on our measure of faith as the woman with the issue of blood; knowing that if we but touch the hem of his garment we will be made whole?

We are to keep our mind stayed on Jesus. In that, we can be confident in the power of the Lord and share our confidence and comfort with others. In sharing with others, we can then help to open their eyes to the word of God. As we share the word, we are then called to pray that the word of God be planted in their heart; that they will be prepared to defeat the enemy and spread the gospel of Jesus Christ.

Lord, when it appears that I am surrounded by the enemy and there's no way out; open my eyes so that I may see.  When it appears that my finances are not going to cover my obligations, please Jesus open my eyes.  When it appears that the doctor's report is getting a bit overwhelming and I can't rest, Lord, open my eyes.  When it appears that all hope is gone and once again I find myself desiring to go astray; to do things my way; Father, open my eyes.  And sweet Jesus, when I am on the brink of comprising my walk with you because I can't see my way through, please open my eyes that I may see that you have your angels already encamped around me!

Be Blessed in the Lord.

Gavis Mosley

# TRUE WORSHIP

Psalms 8:1

O Lord, Our Lord…How excellent is your name in all of the earth. You have set your glory above the heavens!

Lord, I pray that you speak to my heart as I worship.

Lord, I worship you because you are excellent and your name is the name above all names: Even the heavens declare your name. True worship belongs to God our Creator, our redeemer, our Savior. True worship is an individual act of love, respect, appreciation and remembrance of the one and only true living God who we have come to know through his word and our fellowship with him because of his word.

As I journey, today especially, I'm looking around me and I see all sorts of worship. But, is it true worship? Are we honoring and recognizing the one who deserves and seeks it most? I think not. I see different ones entertaining themselves with costumes and make up that reflects their interest, personality and character…and…it's something to think about, to ponder I would say. In the name of fun, where is your worship? And, exactly what it is you are declaring your worship to?

True worship is not defined or limited by time nor place for it lies, it lives within each of us. It lives in our born again state of being. It strives as we remember the one who has given so much so that we may have new life. It strengthens us as we go day to day. It delights us as we walk in peace and righteousness. It continually encourages us as we seek the truth, the word of God. True worship belongs to God. It keeps us.

I worship God as I adore the movement of his creation. The clouds in the sky, as I watch the twinkle of the star, as I hear the rumble of thunder or see the flashes of lightening. The budding of the flowers remind me of new beginning just as the change of the color of leaves from green to orange to brown signify purpose for such a time as this. As those same leaves fall to the ground, I fall as well to my knees to worship God for he is teaching me. He is keeping us.

I worship the Lord God because of his glory and the way he manifest himself in so many ways. He's in the smile of the stranger just as he is in the tear of a friend. He's in the joy of the celebration just as he is in your moments of pain. God is with us as we strive in health just the same as he is with us at the end of our day when we are no more. We're called to worship him.

I thank God for his indwelling of the Holy Spirit, his precious gift to me, it leads and guides me into true worship. It keeps the distractions of life away just long enough that I may worship. It is he who has created a new mind and a pure heart in me. He keeps us.

As we come into the true realization of who God is; we can't help but worship him. We are able to see him at work in all that we do. He has become an integral active and living part of each believer. God is keeping you and he's keeping me.

I worship the Lord because there is none like him. He is holy, righteous and faithful. He is love, mercy, grace and justice. He is the Lord God who does not change. There is none like him. I know him as mighty, wonderful and supreme. I worship him because he is truth and because he reigns. I worship him because he is….the great I AM.

I worship God because in my search for peace and comfort, he is there. As I learn to allow God to have his way, I worship him…there are still times when I just can't find my way, I find that I must let go and let God have his way. Letting go and letting God…easy to say…often hard to do…but as I surrender to my faith…I worship. It is then that I'm called to remember all that he's done for me.

In my worship, things begin to happen. I'm called to remember all the times when I allowed the enemy to make me feel inadequate, crazy, unworthy. I allowed him to make me feel ashamed. I allowed him to block the spirit of the knowledge of the word of God from my heart. I needed to know that there was no hurt nor sorrow that God could not nor would not heal. I allowed him to stand between the joy of my salvation and the desire of my flesh. But God, he changed all that for me…one fine day. He is my protector, he is my redeemer, and he is my wise counsel. We're called to worship.

I worship because I desire the presence and the power of God. I worship because it is God and God alone who is able to restore me to his delight. It is God who has healed me at a cost that no amount of money would be enough. The life that I live today was paid for with the blood of the son of God. Jesus gave up his divinity for such a time so that he could save a wretch like you and a wretch like me. He came to earth as man, so that he may walk in our shoes, yet remain pure in heart and spirit. It was his love and the love of his Father that allowed him to do the work on the Cross. And work it was, a mighty work. One that allowed water and blood to flow at the same time; one that came to heal a dying world, one that offers salvation, new life, forgiveness, to all who will receive it. The work of Jesus was physically brutal yet it accomplished a spiritual victory. The work of Jesus was so powerful that nature, all creation, beheld as the earth shook and gave way to his spirit all the while he continued to do the work that he had come to do…forgive sin, offer a way to salvation…until that moment came when he lowered his head into his shoulder and cried out to his Father. Life as man knew it would never be the same again. There is a worshiper in us.

I worship because the story did not end there. For my Lord, Jesus rose from a borrowed tomb with all power, I say all power, over all heaven and earth in his hand. All power over all things. It is this power that allows man a chance at new life in Jesus Christ. Restoration power is yours you have only to believe.

He gives me protection from dangers seen and unseen. Knowing the danger that we've seen him keep us from, just consider all the things that you didn't see, you don't even know about…my Lord. It's time to worship him.

Words don't do God justice and they were not intended to. We have but to experience him for ourselves. It's a personal journey, a way that we must all go. Therefore, I really can't express how nor why I worship him fully so that you will understand just how important worship is in the life of the believer but allow me to share one more thing. Worship, in spirit and in truth, pleases God. I desire to please and be pleasing to God and that is reason enough for me. Amen and bless the Lord.

Gavis Mosley

# MEDITATION OF DANIEL

Daniel 9:19  Lord, listen! Lord, forgive! Lord, hear and act! For your sake, my God, do not delay, because your city and your people bear your Name.   Daniel remembered and prayed to the Lord.

There is power in our prayers. Prayer moves the hands of God. In our prayers, we must dare to ask ourselves "Is there anything too hard for God?" We must be faithful in our request, trusting in our heart and sincere in our desire; as, we keep God first.

As a believer, we must know that God is near always. We must stand on the fact that only what we do for God will last.  Our labor for him is not in vain.  We must trust and depend on him for the knowledge and wisdom required to be strengthened along the way. As we consider the journey, we must know God as our Savior, our shepherd, the one who goes before us with all power and authority. Seek God and not man.

Lord, as I think about you…then about my own fragile being…I realize the need to put all my trust in you.  I thank you for the mysteries of your word that you are revealing.  I thank you for the spirit that dwells within for it is truly a gift from you.  It was you who made such a sacrifice for one so undeserving as me. Thank you for your word for as I spend time in it, I desire to be closer to and more like you.

God is blessing me right now! God is doing a great work in me for he is the reason that I am now free! He has kept me for such a time as this, for his work in me is being realized. The work which began as an avenue of acceptance, cleansing and restoration was but a seed, a foundation for the continued uplifting of the kingdom of God. What was once but a dream is soon to become a living vessel as to the greatness of the Lord.

As I consider my journey, my most precious memories are those regarding the beginning, the restoring…of how fragile and insecure I had become. I was so broken and marred. I was angry and disappointed, hurt and ashamed, lonely and lonesome, empty and troubled, sadden and sad…have you ever been there? Have you ever wondered why God was keeping you yet another day? I've been there and it was there that I came to know the Lord in a new and intimate way. Thanks to God, I now rejoice for I can experience the joy of my salvation and worship him in spirit and truth. My strength, assurance, hope, faith, trust and love is founded in the word and work of God.

I'm taken to a study of the prophet Daniel. He had many trials and tribulations to endure. He was taken from his homeland and became a captive in a foreign land as a young man. Daniel was in the land but did not conform to its customs. This was during a time when God allowed the nation of Israel to be taken by the Babylonians because of continued disobedience and idol worship. They had turned their backs on God and refused to worship him.

But Daniel and a devoted few remained faithful; their foundation was the one and true living God.

The word foundation speaks of much. It was Daniel's foundation that kept him during this period (a life time for many) of 70 years. A foundation is what everything else stands on. It bears the responsibility of all that stands above it. It is the underlying principle that holds something together or makes sense of a thing; without it there is no meaning. Because Daniel was founded in the Lord, God granted him favor. He was a captive in the land but he was free as he soared as an eagle in the spirit of the Lord.

Daniel literally spent most of his life in Babylonia. He faced adversity, threats to his life due to his worship; yet, he remained obedient and faithful to God. Year after year, trial after trial, challenge after challenge, enemies here and there, Daniel stood steadfast and unmovable.

70 years later…He remembered the word, the promise of God. He realized that the time has come to release the people of God to return to their homeland. They would return to a land and temple that had been destroyed and that had been in ruins for years. Daniel didn't focus on the negative but he looked to the promise, the word. And then he prayed.

Daniel's prayer of intercession was lifted before the Lord. He began by acknowledging God as great and awesome, as faithful and true to his people in his promises and well as his wrath. He then began to confess not only his sins but those of the people. He confessed the specific wrongs against God one by one. He then reminded God of his promise to his people. He spoke to God not regarding any righteousness of man but spoke to his mercy. He appealed to God's name and his place of worship. He knew that it would be God who would have to be glorified and not man. Man has not righteousness without God. God heard Daniel and blessed his prayer.

There's no greater love than that which answers prayer. We have all had a Babylonian experience. God is the keeper of our souls and it is he who can free us from being captive of the evil one. But we are called to remember, to remember the promises and the word of God.

I love this scripture because it speaks to the importance of our foundation being the Lord. Daniel didn't fold under the pressures and circumstances of life nor did he seek temporary gratification. He remained faithful. I wish I could say that my journey paralleled Daniel's. No, it was not even close. I fell short of the call time and time again. But one fine day, God saw fit that I would remember his promises and his work; I did cry out to the Lord as Daniel did and God heard my cry. He answered my cry, he restored me back to him. My foundation is now the Lord. Come what may, I'm standing on the word of God. I am convinced to hide his word and his ways in my heart, never to be shaken nor moved as before. In his word, he tells me that greater is he who is in me than is in this world. I'm to be in this world not conformed to it. I am more than a conqueror in God. I am the head and not the tail. I am the lender and not the borrowed. I am the redeemer of the Lord. My faith is founded in Jesus Christ.

If the Lord kept a record, a count of our sins, we would not be able to stand, to witness, to love, to serve him, with all our heart, mind and soul. The weight of unforgiven sin would be more than we could bear. That's why we have a Savior, a sinless redeemer, who has done it all…so that we may live eternally with him. Lord, we thank you.

Praise God for he continues to call us into a closer, more personal walk with him. He cares for us and he need us to be obedient to his word. Just as Daniel asked God to restore the people back to Jerusalem, God is waiting for us to come to him acknowledging him as Lord of our lives surrendering our all to him. We need restoration. It is for God's glory and the uplifting of his kingdom.

Life, with God as the foundation, is pleasing. It will be rewarded at the appointed time. In Jesus name, Amen.

Gavis Mosley

# LESSON LEARNED

It has been my experience that God will call you in from your troubles. Yep, he will do that! You may wonder what I mean. It is like this: We are flesh striving daily to live holy. Daily I must, we must, die to this flesh and live in Jesus Christ. As we live in Jesus Christ, he begins to call us out of our sin. We begin to hear his voice in our spirit. When our thoughts begin to wonder, we will often consider "a thing" that will be pleasing to us for a moment.

This is something that would serve to distract us from our normal, sometimes boring routine (by the world's standard). It is something that would not take us away long (so you think) but would surely add some "spice" or "excitement" to our life (another of the world's lies). It would be a well-deserved escape. This one idea is the reason why God calls us to have a renewed mind, a new way of considering things in Jesus Christ. Satan is planting a seed of unrighteousness in our spirit. We know that our thoughts or ideas are not a part of our chosen walk in the Lord, yet, it is so appealing for the moment. It becomes an overpowering thought that we have just got to do it (we are no longer yielding to the Holy

Spirit but to the desires of the flesh) and do it right now. (Is it too late to say, "Help, Holy Ghost?") Ever so softly a voice speaks "no, don't do that, it will only serve to distract you from your purpose, your progress, your walk with me." This is the voice of God calling you out of your moment of temptation.

Too often, we make the decision to do it anyway and find ourselves in a "mess" we never thought possible. We find ourselves in a place we know we should not be; yet, we have allowed our thoughts to manifest into action. Again, the voice of the Lord speaks, "okay, my child, now enough is enough, come on back in." Well, by now, it's feeling good and we have determined in our weak, sick, and deprived mind that what we are doing, it not that bad a thing after all. We begin to rationalize our actions and minimize our sin as we seek to find peace in this act of disobedience. As we journey, we must learn that our flesh is never satisfied; it requires more and more.

It may be a lifestyle of telling lies, drugs, alcohol, cheating, stealing, and jealousy, back-biting or even adultery. It really does not matter what the thing is but it does matter what we decide to do about it. I will say, the sooner we are able to call on God to help us; the sooner we will be restored to our rightful place in him. The longer the flesh is being gratified; we buy into Satan's lie that just a little more won't be so bad. The lie that I am doing okay and I can stop when I get ready. This lie is followed by: I am going to stop tomorrow. God will call you out for he will send a word to you that tomorrow may be too late. (The word of God says no one knows neither the day nor the hour that he will return. It also says that we are not promised tomorrow.) The lie that nobody really cares about what we are doing. The biggest lie of all is that nobody knows; it's a secret. Just in case you forgot or didn't get the memo: We serve a living all-knowing God.

The tempter will come to you with only those things that will hinder you. He's not going to tempt you with what appeals to someone else because he knows that you will resist it. We must know that he knows the desires of the flesh, my flesh, your flesh. He can only tempt us at our weakness. I say to you and to myself, accept your weakness. Give it to God. At such time, we can be strong in God and the power of his might. God will call you out. Don't compare your shortcomings or failures to another person's. (We have all fallen short of the glory and pleasing will of God.) This is a trick of Satan; because in doing so we don't look "so bad." This concept excuses us to stay in our sin just a little bit longer. The longer we stay in sin, the more okay it becomes. (But, in the life of a child of God, the Holy Spirit is grieved and there is no peace, no sleep, and no joy.) We have been deceived by the master deceiver and his voice is speaking to us with boldness and clarity. We are having a prodigal son experience.

For you see, he too became bored with life. He was raised with the gift of family, love and the Lord. Satan gave him a "Polaroid snapshot" (a look at instant pleasure) of life away from home (God). (It is God who holds the portrait, the final finished picture of a life developed over time with him.) The son went to his father one day; and, asked that he be given his inheritance that he may venture out in to the world and really live the "good life." As a loving father would do, he was granted his request. (Know that God will not make us serve him. He allows us to come to him freely. It is his goodness and love that draws us to him not his strong arm.)

As the story goes, he left home and got his party started. He found himself quite a popular lad, handsome, and full of charm. Friends and fun (Satan's smoking gun) were his desire. Well, when his fortune ran out (as things of the world do) so did everything and everyone. He wondered what he must do. Well, he was still a good worker, so he found himself a job, and thought that he would be okay. (Don't you know that you are nothing and cannot prosper without the Lord being on your side?) By now, he was in the very clutch of Satan. Instead of things getting better, they grew worse. He was no longer himself, the same youngster who had just left his father's house. Depression and rejection were now his friends. But God, one day, he was called out, as he was hungry for restoration, redemption, forgiveness, love and acceptance. The word of God says that he came back to himself. (We are urged to train up our children in the ways of God so that they will not depart from it.) He desired to return home (to God). He gathered enough of himself to walk out of shame, guilt, pity and disobedience to go back home. Look at God.

While he was yet afar off, his father saw him and began to prepare for his "homecoming". The son had to accept his disobedience before he could accept his forgiveness and be restored. He had to be reminded of the goodness of his father. As the story goes, he was received wholeheartedly by his father (as we are as we return to our heavenly father.) He was restored to his rightful place.

Because of who you are Lord: I give you honor and glory. Is

it not awesome how: God (our Father) does not give up on us? He waits patiently for our return. God will allow us to live in our sin but when our hearts turn to him, he will renew us. He will give us a new walk and a new talk. He asks only that we believe so that we may receive.

God desires that we come home to him. We must know that we can't get so "lost" that Jesus will not find us. It is good to remember: When the world says that it is all over, your journey with God has just begun.

Lord, I thank you for being who you are in my life today. You are my provider. You are my counsel. You are my victory. You are my prince of peace. I worship you because of who you are. You are my creator. You are my hope. Be blessed in the Lord.

Gavis Mosley

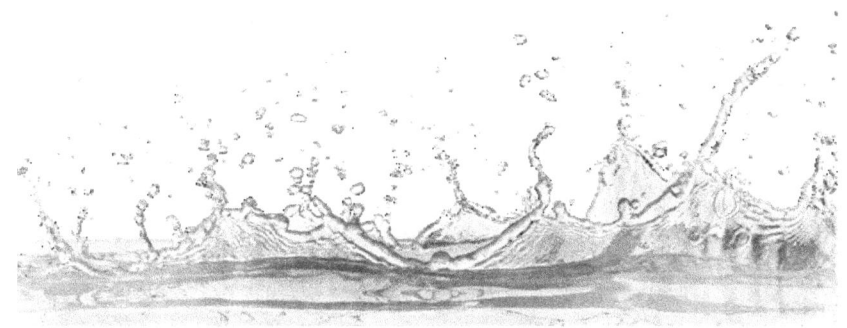

# I'M AFRAID

It's me, it's me Oh Lord! Standing here, right here, in the need of prayer! Learning to lean on Jesus is learning to live out my faith. My faith cries out…In the day of trouble, of change, of uncertainty, of newness. I will seek the Lord.

God knows just what's going on in my life. With this, he knows, if I'm placing my faith and my hope in him. When I speak of faith, I speak of an honest hope and trust, a unique reliance and an assurance. It deals with my personal and most intimate relationship with God. Today, for me, it deals with the fact that I know that God knows me, for he created me. In that, he has a deep knowledge of my being. And today as I face my crossroad of circumstance, I know that He knows when I'm at rest in him and when I'm struggling in his way. That's why I say, as I stand before you Lord, I stand in the need of prayer. For it is I who knows you and who has the upmost faith in you…I am afraid.

I am being called to go through something and I don't want to do it. I don't.

At the center of the issues of life, lies the heart of the man. So your heart is, your issue will be also. As I journey, one thing has proven itself to be true, all my beginnings and all my ends lie in what I believe, in where my faith lies not in myself but in my savior and redeemer…Jesus Christ.

Lord I need you to speak to my heart. I need you to calm my soul. I've got an issue, a crossroad, a Red Sea that I must walk through, that I must decide which way to go, that I must cross. It's one that has been in the making, one that I've been able to manipulate and control, one that I have had the opportunity and privilege to put off. It is one that I have chosen to ignore because I could. It is one in which Mother Nature and Father Time were in a race to the finish line and I was dutiful in holding the reins. Needless to say, as life would have it, the reins have been shifted and I am now called to honor and respect the fact that both were created by God and I am being called into obedience, submission! It's interesting. I know that in change God wants to be pleased with not only with how I react to the change but also in what I'm going to take from the change. It is his desire that I trust him and depend on him through the change knowing that he will work whatever it is for my good. In all change, God deals with us in a personal way. And today, he's dealing with me! In his dealing with me I must admit that there is fear. I know that fear is not from God but the fact remains that I do feel this way. I long for the voice of comfort and assurance.

I've been listening to the wrong report. There are some changes that I must make. There are adjustments to be made and they must be done right now. There is a call for cooperation and understanding that seems to be being ignored. There is a call to surrender and submit to the common good that seems to go unrealized. Even with me, there is a battle raging within between the flesh and the spirit of God. (I need to worship) Thus, there is a call for the reconciliation of the hearts of man, a change must come and for this cause, it must begin with and within me! (I need to worship).

Just as I have realized that which is going on in me, I must have patience and respect for those who are experiencing their time of change as well. I also know that my focus is in the wrong place. I'm too busy worrying about them and them and this thing that is coming against me and not once have I really prayed to God. Not once, have I fallen on my knees and asked God to be with me. Not once have I admitted to God just how I feel. Not once, have I admitted to God that at the center of my issue and moving forward is fear.

Yet as I journey…I do love the Lord…I seek the counsel of those around me. They share their experience, strength and hope and all that has been well and fine. But none of that has given me the peace and assurance that my soul and my spirit needs to truly move forward in confidence and obedience. For you see, at the end of the day, when it is just me, the Lord and this issue, there is no peace, no rest, no joy, and no assurance. None. (Because I have failed to worship.) (I need to worship). I've found myself going through the motions, becoming broken and tired.

In the midst of it all, I sought the encouragement of a sister in Christ. She texted me these words, "My belief is God did not bring you to it to not take you through it." (I began to worship) Then and only then was I able to truly process not just physically but spiritually what was really going on with me. I was allowing my issue to speak to my God. All the confusion that I was experiencing was due to my own making. For it was I who was not operating in the spirit, the truth, the victory, the boldness, the assurance that I knew existed for me in God. It was I who had opened the door for the enemy to come in and set up camp for I had not, and was not acknowledging God and the power of his might in this issue. I was allowing fear to take the place of hope. I had failed to worship in the very beginning of the news of change. Oh, what a difference it would have made. Oh, what a difference it would have made. I've been miserable, desolate, lacking and alone…all because I had failed to worship. Forgive me Lord. But I do know now, for such a time as this, I am called to remember that you are the center of my joy.

You are my God. You are the God of my good and my bad. You are the God of my happy and my sad. You are the God of my familiar and my change. You are the God of my plenty and of my lack. You are the God of my peace and of my doubt. You are the God of all my concerns. You are the God of my worship. In my worship, is perspective, spiritual perspective…revelation, realization…of truth. My identity in Christ began to speak to me and come forth. Victory, More than a conqueror, the head and not the tail, the lender and not the borrower, servant of God, redeemed of the Lord; my identity began to rise above my circumstance. For you see, I was focused on my worship. I blessed the Lord for being my banner for he had already gone before me and prepared the way. He was there waiting for me to call out to him with a sincere heart and a broken spirit. He needed me to be useable. He needed me to worship him. I know now that this change is for God to do a work in me and from it I am already blessed for as I walk through the very shadow of death, I will fear no evil, hurt, harm or danger for my God is with me. His rod and his staff will comfort, lead and guide me.

He is taking me to a new place, a new dependence, a new relationship, a deeper understanding of him as Lord. Because I worshipped, he has wiped away my tears and taken captive my fears. As I worship…The doors may seem like they are closing, but I praise the God of the door. The end may appear as though it will overtake you, but I worship the God of the new beginning. The change may come in such a way that confusion becomes great, but I serve a God of peace and comfort. The name of the Lord is a fortified (protected, strong, sustaining, empowered) tower.

Lord I thank you for the healing faith of the woman with the issue of blood. I thank you for the courage of a giant slayer. I thank you for the victory over the fire in the furnace. I thank you for come what may, you continue to make me better and not bitter. I thank you most for your Son, Jesus Christ. For it is my hope, trust and faith in Jesus that leads me to worship your holy and precious name. I hear you speaking Amen to my issue Lord. It is in such a time as this when I am weak you are strong. It is at such a time as this that when I am listening to the report of man that you will send a quiet, gentle spirit my way that will speak peace to my soul, so that I will hear your voice and your word.

As you whisper ever so softly, "My child, is there anything too hard for your God." I worship you Lord. At the end of this day, I am no longer afraid. I will look unto the hills from which comes all my help, all of my help comes from the Lord. And No. There' nothing too hard for my God!

# HOW DEEP IS YOUR LOVE?

We worship God because of our love for him. We must in our worship thank and adore God for who he is. We must openly proclaim yes to his will and yes to his way. Our worship for God must be real. If your life has changed; then you know that God could have walked away a long time ago, he could have just left you to die, but he did not. God first loved us through the death of his own, so that we might live and love him. Oh how, I ask, how could it be that we would not love him? God has promised that we are never alone; he has given us his word and his holy spirit to live within us as assurance and for guidance; he has left us with the comforter. God's love and our love for him is the strength we need when we fall; it is this love relationship that enables us to get back up again. Our love for God should not allow us to stay in a fallen state. God's love for us restores us. It reminds us that it not too late. God's mercy and grace calls us to love him.

We are called to love God because he is for us. God believes in us. He made us in his very image. God created us to be more than we will ever be able to visualize or realize in the natural.

My friend, I encourage you, I request of you to lay down all that which is not holy, for the love of the Lord. For you see, the love of the Lord has seen me through many troubles and situations, it has allowed me to experience joy, unspeakable joy, it has watched over me and held me, it has spoken to my spirit and awaken a passion in me. And today because of this, I chose to love God because he first loved me.

In the natural, there's nothing like truly falling in love with someone who is already head over heels for you. It is a relationship that is so easy to nourish and appreciate. That person is there when you need them. They are your shoulder to cry on and your partner to share in your joy. They make themselves available for counsel and are a source of inspiration. You share moments that are tender to the heart. You hold hands and occasionally do your own personal and private dance. If you think this makes you have goose pimples and feel good…what more can you imagine in the spiritual regarding the love of God? God's love for me goes much deeper than any man can know or show. We, as humans, cannot express the love of God. For the times when man cannot be found, I can depend on the love of God. For the times when man has let me down, I can depend on the love of God. For all those secrets that I cannot keep, I can depend on the love of God. He is always there…I cannot make it without him on my side. He is my strength and my source. I believe God. I know that his word is true and it is that, and only that, I can truly depend. It will never fail me and I understand that never is a long, long time.

Mark 12: 30-31 reads, "And thou shalt love the Lord thy God with all thy heart and with all they soul, and with all thy mind, and with all thy strength: this is the first commandment…thou shalt love thy neighbor as thyself. There is none other commandment greater than these." I ask you, "How deep is your love?"

Our love for God is at the center of our relationship with him. It is all that truly matters in life. Our love for our neighbor, mankind, is shown when and only when we love God. For the believer, there will be no question as to who we consider our neighbor, we know because of our love for God.

The word says, "Thou shall love the Lord thy God," not that I might, it says that I will love the Lord. I am called to love him and put him before all things. Then it tells me how I should love him, "with all thy…" means I am to give him my all and hold back nothing from him. I am to love "with all my mind…" I can only do this by knowing him. I must study his word and meditate on it day and night. I must. I love God as I come into the full knowledge of him. I am called to love him "with all my heart…" I must have a true deep and sincere affection and passion for God. I must stand and not waiver in my love for him. I must be steadfast and unmovable. I am called to love God "with all my soul…" To love God with all my soul is to love him unto death. For to die in Christ, I must know will be my gain. I must love God "with all my strength…" This says I must love God with all I have. I must use my everything…ability, gifts, money, and time…in the glorifying and uplifting of him.

How do I know that I am loving God as he has called? 1 John 4:20 reads, "If a man say, I love God, and hateth his brother, he is a liar: for he that loveth not his brother whom he hath seen, how can he love God whom he hath not seen?" If I love God like I say I do then I will love my neighbor. Then I may ask, "Who is my neighbor?" Read the word of God in Luke 10 where you see the parable of the Good Samaritan. My neighbor is anyone whom I encounter, anyone who needs me. To love my neighbor, I need more of you and less of me. To love our neighbor as we love ourselves is a mighty tall calling because…some of us don't love ourselves…some of us love ourselves so much that we can't see doing what we do for self for someone else…OUCH! True love for God calls us into balance as we are called to love others. Loving others is evidence that we love God. I ask you in conclusion, "Just how deep is your love?"

Be blessed in the Lord.

# WON'T YOU COME?

"Won't you come?" An invitation. A request. A thought that we have all considered. "Won't you come and will you do it today for tomorrow may very well be too late?" "I'm not ready." "I've got to get myself together." "I'm thinking about it." "I'm tired, I need to get my rest." "I don't have a way or anything to wear." Excuses for why not to accept the invitation, for being in a place to accept/receive the invitation to eternal life.

I'm so grateful that I know someone who's able. He's able to do just what he says he will do. I know someone who's bigger than the universe because he created the universe. I know someone who is mightier than the lion, the king of the jungle, for he made the jungle. I know someone who celebrates life with you for he is the center of joy, that is, if you allow him to be.

Who is like the Lord? Take time out today, as a matter of fact, right now, to think on this all important question. Take the time that he has granted you, take the mind that he has regulated for you; take the eyes through which he has blessed you with vision so that you can see, take the heart that he can change for you, and consider for just a moment: Who is like the Lord?

Let's look to who God says he is…the all-knowing, all

powerful, fixer of broken pieces, healer of all sickness and diseases, and ever-present God says this of himself in Isaiah 44: 6-8, "Thus says the Lord, the King of Israel and his Redeemer, the Lord of hosts: I am the first and I am the last, And there is no God besides Me. "Who is like Me? Let him proclaim and declare it: Yes, let him recount it to Me in order. From the time that I established the ancient nation. And let them (the idols) declare to them (the world) the things that are coming and the events that are going to take place. 'Do not tremble and do not be afraid: Have I not long since announced it to you and declared it? And you are my witnesses, is there any God besides Me? Or is there any other Rock? I know of none."

Colossians 1:16 "For by Him all things were created, both in the heavens and on earth, visible and invisible, whether thrones or dominions or rulers or authorities---all things have been created through Him and for Him."

God challenges all other gods to stand up and show themselves to be true. He calls them to do as he has done, confirm the righteous way of man and the path that he must take. Console the soul of man in such a way that he should not doubt. Then show man, reveal to him (God) and man his record of victory. God asks us "can the idol do this?" If so, show it to him. God asks that the idol set the plan of life in order as he has done, from the rising of the sun to the setting of the sun, day after day, and all the day long. Then he says, do not be afraid. I think this is for us. He doesn't want us to be afraid to be his witness as we are called to boldly defend our God before the idol god. God declares that he is our Rock, thus he is who he says he is. He is the one who saves us.

Again, it is God as our Rock who saves us from a dying world so that we will have eternal life in him. No other god can do this for us. When we accept Jesus Christ as our Lord and Savior; we are acknowledging that we have faith in God and that we believe in him and what the word has to say about him. We believe that he is the son of God and that he is the one and only way by which God will accept us into his kingdom.

We, then, walk into a life full of the promises of God. We walk into the reality that our daily existence is made possible by the strength and might of the one who sits high and looks low. We learn that trials and temptations come to not break us but to make us strong. We learn that we don't have to worry about the cares, the burdens of life for we have a God who goes before us and he makes all things work for our good.

When we come to God we now have an advocate, he stands in our defense, and he is forever by our side. When the enemy comes against us, we can go to our Lord in prayer and declare and decree our victory in Jesus name. We can hide the word of God in our heart; the enemy may come but he will have to leave. We learn that the battles of life are not for us but that they belong to the Lord. We learn to have faith in those things that we hope for and act accordingly. We learn that the power of life and death lies in the tongue of the believer so long as they line up with the will of God for us. We learn that we can live a righteous life because the spirit of the almighty dwells within us. We learn that our emotions are real but they don't have to overtake us. We have a Father who cares about us and knows just how much we can bear. We come to know God as protector, for he encamps his angels all around us as we go to and fro. It is he who protects us from dangers seen and unseen. We come to know God as one who provides. God is the one who can take little and make much, for he made all things. God is the father of the broken hearted. It is in his bosom that you will find rest. Our faith begins and ends in him. He is the only person who can move man from a hateful heart and contrite spirit to a joyous praise.

Who do you know that you can call on in the midnight hour and he's always there... patiently waiting, listening, answering, comforting, healing, providing, watching, confirming, delivering, and never asleep, never tired...who? Who do you know can take the sting out of death and turn it into a celebration of life? I ask you "who is like the Lord"? Is there another one whom we can truly call God? Won't you come?

God is love. God loves us so much that he gave his only Son, so that whosoever believed in him would have eternal life. This is love. Not so much that we loved God but that he loved us. And what can change or keep us from his love, Romans 8:39..."Nor height nor depth, nor anything else in all creation, will be able to separate us from the love of God in Christ Jesus our Lord." With that there's no place we can go to be out of God's presence, for he is there.

Psalms 139 tells me "If I ascend to heaven, You are there; If I make my bed in Sheol, behold, You are there. If I take the wings of the dawn, If I dwell in the remotest part of the sea, Even there you hand will lead me, and your right hand will lay hold of me." God is always near. I ask again, won't you come?

Lord, it is in you that we realize that our life is not our own.

We realize that we belong to you. As we accept the invitation, we are actually accepting you into our life. It is a life where all our faith and trust is in you. When we accept the invitation, we know that you are near in times of celebration as well as in times of struggle. It is your spirit that lives within us that allows us to hear your voice as it leads us, guides us, teaches us, ministers to you, comfort and assures us. It is in you that we will be able to see the rainbow yet while the storm is still raging.

Isaiah 45:22 extends this invitation..."Turn to me and be saved, all you ends of the earth; for I am God and there is no other." Won't you come? You are already blessed in the Lord.

# ABOUT THE AUTHOR

My name is Gavis Mathews Mosley. I am a resident of West Point, MS. I am a 1978 graduate of West Point High School. In the spring of 1982, I received a bachelor's degree in Radio/TV Broadcasting with a minor in Journalism from Mississippi University for Women located in Columbus, MS. While attending "The W", I was honored to be a charter member of the Omicron Epsilon Chapter of Delta Sigma Theta Sorority Inc.in the fall of 1981. I am a chapter member of the Clay County Alumnae Chapter of which I have been a member since 1983. I have had a varied career path that has ranged from education to work in the radio and television industry to working in a manufacturing environment.

I am the mother of two beautiful daughters, and I am a very proud grandmother. God has shown his favor in my life for I have the awesome privilege to enjoy the company of my mother, and my gem of a grandmother who is 97 years young. Oh, yes, it is by God's grace that we stand 5 generations strong!

It is she, my grandmother, who continued to ask, "What are you going to do with all that stuff you are writing?" The seed was then planted that she would live to see the manifestation of a precious gift. I have always scribbled nuggets on paper, some I kept, some I discarded, for at the time they were just memos that I wrote to me…expressions, inner revelations, fears, doubts and dreams.

I began writing in May 2012 as a freelance faith page writer for the Daily Times Leader and the Starkville Daily News. I am currently an active member of a local church where I teach Sunday School and write "Pastoral Notes" which are printed on the church bulletin.

I enjoy reading, writing and cooking (although I'm not so good at it). My most precious moments are when it's quiet, when everything just stops, the noise and distractions of life come to a rest. My favorite time of the day is in the beginning, early mornings, before the noise. It is there that I find inner peace and assurance in yet another day to walk with the Lord.

www.ingramcontent.com/pod-product-compliance
Lightning Source LLC
Chambersburg PA
CBHW052047070526
44584CB00017B/2084